IMMEASURABLY

Cris is an ordained minister in the Church of England and leads All Hallows Church, Bow, East London which he and his wife planted in 2010. Cris teaches at most of the major British Christian festivals each year and has authored a number of books with the most recent being *The Bible Book by Book* and *Practising Resurrection*.

"What you have here is a book that scratches an itch, in a gentle yet stirring narrative that challenges and provokes. Cris leads us on a journey to lift our eyes above the horizon, to go on a journey of ever-increasing wonder, to look for a deeper well of the Spirit in our own lives and life of the church. The need to expand our imagination and thirst for a deeper experience with an unfathomable God is communicated beautifully in this book. It is a pathway to more, but not a selfish more! – more of the life we have always dreamed of, a life of depth and an encounter with a God who wants to take us further than we could ever imagine."

— **Brian Heasley**, National Director of 24-7 Prayer, UK

"This is a beautiful book by a remarkable leader exploring a magnificent theme. I commend it wholeheartedly to anyone thirsty for more from God."

— **Pete Greig**, 24-7 Prayer / Emmaus Rd / Alpha International

"Cris Rogers is one of the church's creative pioneers with a passion to communicate the Christian faith."

— **Nicky Gumbel**, Alpha

"God wants to completely blow your mind and lead you into the deeper waters of knowing and experiencing him. Trust me, there is so much more than the life which you are currently settling into. Allow this modern day prophet to take you on a journey to discover the One who cannot be contained. It's time to wake up and surrender to the life awaiting!"

— **Rob Peabody**, Awaken

"If God says there's more, it must be true. As Cris shows us, a disappointing experience of Christianity isn't possible, unless you've yet to discover the real thing. I thoroughly enjoyed this book – and it looks really fresh!"

— **Paul Harcourt**, New Wine Regional Director for London and East, and Vicar of All Saints' Woodford Wells

"This is a great book. Cris inspires us to throw aside our blinkered view of Christ and open ourselves to the possibility of the impossible. I for one am praying fervently for MORE HOLY SPIRIT."

— **Virginia Luckett**, UK Churches Team Director, Tearfund

IMMEASURABLY more

TO A DEHYDRATED CHURCH, JESUS
HAS IMMEASURABLY MORE TO OFFER

CRIS ROGERS

Published by Monarch Books (an imprint of Lion Hudson plc)
Wilkinson House, Jordan Hill Road, Oxford OX2 8DR, England
Email: monarch@lionhudson.com www.lionhudson.com/monarch
and by Elevation (an imprint of the Memralife Group)
Memralife Group, 14 Horsted Square, Uckfield, East Sussex TN22 1QG
Tel: +44 (0)1825 746530; Fax +44 (0)1825 748899;
www.elevationmusic.com

ISBN 978 0 85721 637 3
e-ISBN 978 0 85721 638 0

First edition 2015

Acknowledgments
Unless marked otherwise, Scripture quotations are taken from the Holy Bible, New International Version Anglicised. Copyright © 1979, 1984, 2011 Biblica, formerly International Bible Society. Used by permission of Hodder & Stoughton Ltd, an Hachette UK company. All rights reserved. "NIV" is a registered trademark of Biblica. UK trademark number 1448790. Scripture quotations marked "MSG" are taken from *The Message*, copyright © 1993, 1994, 1995, 1996, 2000, 2001, 2002. Used by permission of NavPress Publishing Group. Scripture quotations marked "NLT" are taken from the Holy Bible, New Living Translation, copyright © 1996, 2004. Used by permission of Tyndale House Publishers, Inc., Carol Stream, Illinois 60188. All rights reserved. Scripture quotations marked "KJV" are from The Authorized (King James) Version: rights in the Authorized Version in the United Kingdom are vested in the Crown. Reproduced by permission of the Crown's patentee, Cambridge University Press. Scripture quotations marked "ESV" are taken from The ESV® Bible (The Holy Bible, English Standard Version®), copyright © 2001 by Crossway. Used by permission. All rights reserved. Scripture quotations marked "CEV" are taken from the Contemporary English Version, copyright © 1991, 1992, 1995 by American Bible Society, used by permission. Scripture quotations marked "HCSB" are taken from the Holman Christian Standard Bible (HCSB), copyright © 1999, 2000, 2002, 2003, 2009 by Holman Bible Publishers, Nashville, Tennessee. All rights reserved. Scripture quotations marked "NASB" are taken from the NEW AMERICAN STANDARD BIBLE®, Copyright © 1960, 1962, 1963, 1968, 1971, 1972, 1973, 1975, 1977, 1995 by The Lockman Foundation. Used by permission.

Further acknowledgments on page 271 and in notes.

Every effort has been made to trace copyright holders and to obtain permission for the use of copyright material. The publisher apologizes for any errors or omissions and would be grateful to be notified of any corrections that should be incorporated in future reprints of this book.

A catalogue record for this book is available from the British Library

Printed and bound in Poland, January 2015, LH44

Design by Sublime.
design@sublimelive.com

NOW TO HIM WHO IS ABLE TO DO **IMMEASURABLY MORE** THAN ALL WE ASK OR IMAGINE, ACCORDING TO HIS POWER THAT IS AT WORK WITHIN US, TO HIM BE GLORY IN THE CHURCH AND IN CHRIST JESUS THROUGHOUT ALL GENERATIONS, FOR EVER AND EVER! AMEN.

Ephesians 3:20–21

CONTENTS

FOREWORD

In 1952 C. S. Lewis wrote to *The Times* calling for a "Deep Church", a rediscovery and return to the historic foundations laid by Christ and the Apostles, rather than the superficial thin veneer religion characteristic of much modern Christianity. Two generations on, we still need to heed this prophetic call and return to the deep things of God.

A few years ago we had a family holiday in Normandy.[1] One morning I spent time with the Lord and sensed him say he was going to reveal something significant to me. I recorded this impression in my journal and went into the day expectant. We had a great family day visiting the sublime Mont St Michel, but no divine revelation came. On returning, Tiffany and my sons went to feed the aged giant Koi carp in the pond at the bottom of the garden, and I lay on my bed in the late balmy afternoon, musing on the day and wondering if I had missed the Lord's promised revelation. Suddenly my wife Tiffany's voice called out anxiously "Simon, come quick, there's a fish in trouble."

I rushed to the end of the garden and there, stuck in the mud in a few inches of water, was a massive orange, black, and silver carp with a girth like a sumo wrestler. Why it had swum into the shallow end I don't know – perhaps this was a favourite spot and the fish hadn't reckoned on the abnormally hot weather, coupled with the low rainfall, resulting in the sinking of the water level. The pond was half its usual depth and this noble fish didn't have enough water. Trying to wriggle back towards safer depths, this fish embedded itself in the sand, gills partly above water, slowly suffocating to death. I climbed into the pond, perched on an exposed stone, and tried to gently nudge the fish with a stick towards deeper water – but this probably only annoyed my fish and ultimately proved futile. I asked Tiffany to fetch a dustbin lid and a watering can and she ran off and quickly returned with them. Pouring the water on the fish offered momentary relief, then I lifted the fish onto the dustbin lid, carried it to the deep end and lowered it gently in. We held our breath as the fish lay there in the water motionless, fighting for its breath. Then it suddenly seemed to lunge to life; with a swish of its tail and a cocky splash, it found its balance and with a flash of orange, black, and silver turned and swam for the deep end. The family all applauded with delight and relief.

Immediately I sensed the Lord speaking to my mind: "The Church is like that carp: mature, distinguished, and impressive. She has lived long, fought hard, eaten well. But she has been lured out of the deep waters. And she is stuck in the mud and suffocating. Occasional momentary relief from a spiritual watering can will not save her. Her only hope is to get back to the deeps." This was the revelation God had wanted to tell me – his heart's concern for his Church in distress, out of her depth, dying in the shallows. That evening my instantly recognizable orange, black, and silver carp was seen playing around in the deep end – but tragically its fellow fish had not learnt from its lesson and my family was gutted when on successive days we returned to find other fish making the same mistake. Without help to hand, they lay dead in the shallow end mud.

Immeasurably More is a call and a map back to the deep end – its author understands the church's need for depth and direction out from the shallows into authentic Christianity. This book is not a sharp prod with a religious stick, nor a momentary shower with a spiritual watering can; it is a biblically grounded, Christ centred and practically applied guide to live fully and fruitfully for Jesus. *Immeasurably More* is a serious call to glorious discipleship. There is nothing new here – we don't need it, because quite frankly the old is better – nothing fluffy, nothing faddish, nothing hyped. This is simply vintage Christian living, reminding us of our foundations, directing us along old paths, challenging us to lay hold of that for which Christ laid hold of us, and inspiring us in the great adventure of faith.

Rev Simon Ponsonby
Pastor of Theology, St Aldates, Oxford, author of *God Is For Us*

THE WORLD IS PERISHING FOR LACK
OF THE KNOWLEDGE OF GOD
AND THE CHURCH IS FAMISHING
FOR WANT OF HIS PRESENCE.
A. W. Tozer

INTRODUCTION: THE BEGINNING...

HERE

We start our journey on a beach. As we watch the waves breaking on the shore, we realize that there is so much more before us. There is life under the surface of the sea, there is life beyond the limit of the horizon, and there is life hidden above the clouds in the sky; there is so much more than we can see, taste, or imagine. Sadly, we have limited ourselves to the beach and we behave as though this beach is all we have. And it is true that there is a great deal for us to appreciate in this present moment and place, much that we still haven't valued or experienced right here in the familiar, but that doesn't stop us from exploring the great unknown out there.

The God of the Scriptures is the God who has placed us on the beach, but He offers us so much more than just the sand we stand on. The sea rolls open before us, and beyond that there is more than we could ever imagine. We are invited to experience the more with God, and not just to be content with the place we're inhabiting right now. To set out on an open-sea adventure where we will travel to indescribable lands and receive gifts we never knew even existed. The God of the Scriptures is a God of adventures, including gigantic fish, shipwrecks, giants, and campfires.

So here we are. We have a church that God has graciously given us to enjoy. But the church has in too many cases become satisfied with the small beach and the little bit of sea open before us. We have become too content. I don't want to leave behind a church that is content with merely half an adventure; I want to travel with a church that is daring to go for all the immeasurably more that God has shown and still will show us.

THERE

We are "here" and God wants us to be willing to go "there" with Him; to venture deeper into the sea He has made for us to swim, surf, and sail in.

I think the truth is we need rattling. Our cages are too easy and we are comfortable with what we think we know. We are content with what we have. This stems from our love of safety: we feel secure in our buildings with our nicely polished church leaders.

But Jesus came to rattle the religious.

And, boy, do we still need to be rattled!

RATTLING THE RELIGIOUS

God didn't give us the church to be settled and staid; He gave us the church to be weird, a peculiar people, a holy nation. He wants us to be odd – and happy about it. This is a book about rattling the religious, becoming weird because *His* weird Spirit is in us, encouraging the weary, and digging deep into the wells that have sustained the church for many centuries.

So we stand on the beach and we have a decision to make. Do we carry on as we are, or do we jump into the sea of more, which our Father has created and ordained for us?

Do we sit back and enjoy the view, or do we run forward into the broad vista of more?

DEHYDRATION

Disclaimer: I'm not a sports fan. I wouldn't want you to think the following metaphor has been used because of my love of sport. I've tried running a few times but I've come to the conclusion that it's just not for me. I cycle and walk; you might catch me running up stairs, but you will never find me running for recreation. However, despite that, a few years ago I decided that I would try running as a way of keeping fit during Lent. Rather than forty days of prayer and exercise, it became forty days of prayer and excuses. Lent was early that year and the mornings were still dark, so I decided that I could run undercover without anyone catching me. It backfired slightly, as what I would describe as my early mornings turned out to be other people's late afternoons. Nevertheless, I ran for the whole of one week.

As I said, it wasn't for me.

I started the week by jumping out of bed and heading out for a run before my morning shower. I didn't drink anything before, during, or after my run. I just ran. Within a few days I started to feel achy, dizzy, tired, headachy, and lethargic. This wasn't just because I'd done some exercise; I was becoming dehydrated. I had never felt like this before and it was a strange feeling.

I sometimes think that the church seems like this. Could it be that the church is dehydrated after years of running the race and having failed to tap into the living water and passing by the water points around the track without realizing?

It's been my feeling that some of us are running on low; we have become achy, dizzy, and lethargic. Not lethargic about the message or the beauty of this good news, but lethargic in the race itself. We are done in, on our knees, with dry mouth and parched lips. But this isn't where we have to be and it's certainly not where God wants us to be.

This book isn't going to make you feel exhausted or demand lots from you. God has done all the hard work; that's the Good News! We are now in the position of responding to His hard work and receiving all that He has for us.

MORE

Ephesians 3:20 says: "*Now to him who is able to do immeasurably more...*"

Jesus is the God who is able to do immeasurably more. Some translations say the "God of above and beyond" (HCSB); others have "exceeding abundantly above" (KJV) or "infinitely more" (NLT), and *The Message* reads: "far more than you could ever imagine or guess or request in your wildest dreams".

But we are masters at restricting Jesus. We box Him in. We say, "This is how He works." In response to all our attempts to define, understand, and control Him, Jesus reminds us that He has *"immeasurably more"* to offer His church.

How often do we feel that we are at the end of our energy? Not only physically and emotionally, but also spiritually? Some of us have been running this race for so long that we have become dangerously dehydrated.

Jesus is calling all of us into a *radically empowered life* that we couldn't ever achieve in our own strength. Jesus tells His church that there is immeasurably more on offer than just a religious life, a good life, or a moral life. There is more to offer our families and friends, more to offer our neighbourhoods.

Jesus offers us an immeasurably more powerful and beautiful life.

To a dehydrated church, Jesus announces... MORE is always on offer.

God has more for us to **receive,**
More for us to **become,**
And **further** for us to go.

THE WORD WITHOUT THE SPIRIT,
YOU DRY UP, THE SPIRIT WITHOUT
THE WORD, YOU BLOW UP...
BUT THE WORD AND THE SPIRIT
TOGETHER — YOU GROW UP.
David Watson

Jesus longs for His church not to be fed merely on pithy statements, inspiring tweets, or encouraging sermons. There are some churches that have almost written the Holy Spirit out of the creed. We (don't) believe in the Father, Son, and Holy Bible. Trust me; I'm a Bible teacher! Jesus longs for us to be more *empowered* by His Holy Spirit.

"Empowered" is an interesting word. We think of it as meaning being given physical power, but in fact it refers to being authorized, inspired, and enabled. Jesus wants His church to be authorized to do the work of His kingdom, inspired to dream bigger dreams, and enabled to do this work not under our own steam but under His.

So where do we go from here? How do we leave the land of dehydration for an adventure across open seas, caught up with all that God has to offer us?

Well, for me, that adventure starts with getting **HIGHER**, then **CLOSER**, plummeting **DEEPER**, broadening into **WIDER,** and then being equipped **FURTHER**.

> **QUESTION:** What in life has left you exhausted?

> **QUESTION:** What aspects of faith or church have brought you to the point of dehydration? Are you able to pinpoint the things lacking or weighing heavily on you that have worn you down?

15

Immeasurably Deeper: Small-Group Study

Each chapter concludes with a small-group Bible study consisting of a passage and questions. Whether or not you come up with the "right answers" isn't the point. The hope is that each study will help you and a small group of friends to pause and spend just a little more time on the themes of the chapter.

HE MUST INCREASE, BUT I MUST
DECREASE.

John 3:30 (ESV)

A Higher Story
A real story about a person called Mark

I grew up in Whitechapel, East London, with a longing to fit in and make the most of all that life had to offer. I wanted it all, and didn't care who got in my way. I had this deep yearning to seek money, nice women, nice cars, nice clothes. All of this I wanted as quickly and easily as possible, with the least amount of work on my part. The easiest ways of obtaining all this led me into a life of crime. Craving people to know and like me, all I wanted was to be treated like a celebrity everywhere I went.

This desire led me into gambling, which led on to taking drugs. All I did was seek out the wrong people. I didn't care about good people; I wanted nothing to do with them. I couldn't get anything from them.

What controlled me was what people thought of me; I wanted everyone to like me and think of me as successful. I had to have the best cars and clothes, and without them I felt quite hollow. I thought I was so smart that I could wriggle my way out of anything. When I was first offered a drug I thought it wasn't going to be a big deal. The first time you're offered a drug it isn't by a stranger but by a pal. It's friends who will tell you it's a good idea, and I believed them; the crazy thing is, they thought they were doing me a favour.

It's been my experience that people don't believe in God until something goes wrong, and then it's God's fault. I was in a miserable place of my own choosing, alone and wishing I was dead. I remember screaming up at God to get me out of there. I ended up going to a friend of mine who runs a Christian treatment centre in Bristol, and everything changed when I looked up.

I discovered that I had been so focused on myself that I hadn't realized God was even there. All I could see was what was right in front of me, but when I started to look up higher and higher I realized just how powerful God really was. When I chose to look up I saw something other than myself, and He was just what I needed.

MOVEMENT
ONE
HIGHER

FOR THIS REASON I KNEEL
BEFORE THE FATHER.
Ephesians 3:14

NOW TO HIM WHO IS ABLE TO DO
IMMEASURABLY MORE THAN ALL
WE ASK OR IMAGINE...
Ephesians 3:20

Our first movement is "Higher". Within this section I have identified three particular failings that we may have with regard to God. There are times when we can make Him too small, a miniature pocket God whom we carry around; there are times when we lose our sense of wonder at the amazing Creator God and reduce His power; and there are times when we are at risk of being too familiar with Him, treating Him like a "mate" rather than acknowledging His power and might.

1 A MINIATURE GOD

A TSUNAMI OF A GOD

A friend of mine named James had from his teenage years a burning desire to tell people about the Good News. This started when he first encountered God's presence. It was as if he realized that God's love was the most overwhelming, wild, uncontrollable, holy, untameable, and raging love, yet at the same time so gentle, pure, merciful, and compassionate, and he knew he needed to tell people about it.

This God that he first met wasn't a God who was anything like us, even though we can try to understand Him as such. This God was far more powerful, more loving, more frightening, more gracious, more peaceful, more tender, more just, more holy, more glorious, more thrilling, more infinite, more exciting.

This God he met couldn't be summed up by neat doctrinal statements; He was just too awe-inspiring. Too gob-smacking. Too infinite. Too, too, too... Words couldn't and can't contain Him.

It was this God that he showed me, and it is this God that I hope to show others.

A God that makes us go "WOW".

This sense of "WOW" is what powers our worship, our desire for His presence, and makes us realize we are sinful, bitter people who need His grace. It's this untameable tsunami of God's wrath and mercy that draws us into His loving arms and then into the realization that we can actually know this God.

It is this that makes us kneel before Him and look up higher than we have looked before. J. I. Packer puts it beautifully when he writes, "What makes life worthwhile is having a big enough objective, something which catches our imagination and lays hold of our allegiance, and this the Christian has in a way that no other person has. For what higher, more exalted, and more compelling goal can there be than to know God?"[1]

From the earliest years of life on earth, human beings have had a desire to kneel before something. We are made with a deep longing inside us to worship the sacred, and for many that involves finding their own gods. Farming communities would worship the soil, rain, wind, and sun as powerful entities that were able to bring either blessing or curse on their land. Other societies would place small clay "gods" or figurines on shelves around their homes to watch over them and keep them safe as long as they were worshipped. It was a simple transaction: if you kept the gods happy, then the gods would keep you happy. Please the clay god by worshipping it and the clay god will give you all you need.

Farmers would take their small clay gods out of the house and into the fields, and pray that they would bless the land so that it would produce more crops. Sometimes, in order to attract a god's attention and particularly to increase the yield of his crops, a farmer might hire a young girl from the village and have sex in the field, thus pleasing his fertility god. It was like porn for the gods. One Middle Eastern clay god was called Baal, later becoming known as *Ba'al Zəbûb* or, as we say, Beelzebub, and referred to by Jesus as the devil in Matthew 12:27.

From the dawn of time the devil has tricked people into trying to satisfy their longing to connect with the divine, that innate desire to worship God, by worshipping the things that God created. People have even had "pocket gods", which were used as a type of lucky charm to keep the day ticking over nicely.

How archaic!
How barbaric!
How... like us are they?

It is true that we don't have little clay models over our doors or on our shelves that we worship and give food or drink to; however, it is also true that all too often we find ourselves putting other things in the place of God: relying on other things to bring us peace, fortune, and success and to satisfy that desire within us to worship and adore something. The clay gods of our society include the plastic and metal computer devices that help organize our days, contact our mothers, and connect little blobs of candy in mobile games. We love to worship created stuff, be it fashion, our bank accounts, our homes, our children, our position in society, celebrities, or technology. We have magazines that act like Bibles as they help us navigate through life, taking advantage of the small gods around them. We are so dependent on being liked that we surround ourselves with things that measure how many friends we have.

Could it be that we are no different from the ancestors who worshipped clay gods in homes, fields, and town squares? The desire is still within us; we just react to it differently.

But — I hear you say — we are the ones in the church; we *know* that the yearning within us to worship something was placed there by God, and we gather to worship Him. We know Him and we spend time with Him!

That's true. However, if I were to ask you to describe the God you worship, perhaps to draw the God you spend time with, what would it look like?

Try to imagine His holiness. Try imagining His character. Try to imagine His infinitude.

A major challenge we have on Sunday in church is to avoid blaspheming God from our pulpits. It's not through a lack of confidence in the gospel, or necessarily a faulty concept of grace, but by our human tendency to worship a god that is significantly smaller than the God who is revealed in the Bible.

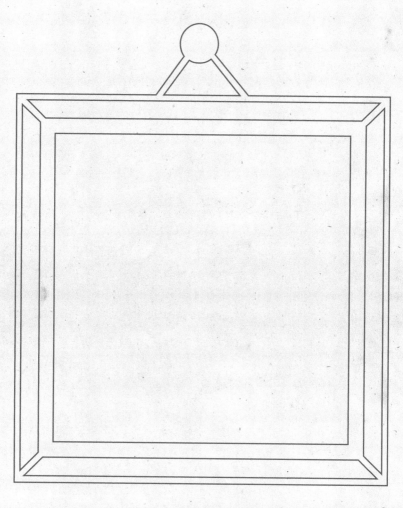

Draw what you imagine God to be like. Are you able to depict His qualities, His character, and His immensity?

It is incredibly hard to draw or even to picture God. Inevitably, the image of God that we have is infinitely too small, feeble, and insignificant, and therefore in danger of being demeaning to Him. Whatever our highest thoughts and ideas of God are, they can never do justice to His greatness. Our own imaginations fail us; they just will not let us create a mental image big enough. This is the brilliance of God; our imagination can't fathom His greatness, beauty, and wonder. That is why Paul is quick to confess, "How unsearchable are His judgments and unfathomable His ways! For who has known the mind of the Lord, or who became His counselor?"[2]

However, instead of trying to stretch our understanding to fit this image of God, all too often we content ourselves with the smaller and safer image. We create a miniature version of God, in many ways like the clay gods, although this one looks God-shaped but isn't quite as big.

A. W. Tozer, an American author and preacher, writes, "When we try to imagine what God is like we must of necessity use that-which-is-not-God as the raw material for our minds to work on; hence whatever we visualise God to be, He is not, for we have constructed our image out of that which He has made and what He has made is not God."[3]

In using the "created" to form our image of God, our human tendency is to shrink Him down to a manageable, unthreatening size. It's easily done, but can be so harmful to our relationship with Him. We need to challenge our miniature God and refocus our eyes, as best we can, on the limitless, almighty, massive God.

To accomplish this we need to return to the Scriptures and regain a sense of wonder and awe at the almighty God. The Scriptures are full of wonder and only ever speak of God in this way. As we read and study them, we realize that although they try to show us God they can only ever give us a hint, a nudge, a flicker of an image. They point towards Him but we only ever see a part of Him, an aspect of Him; we can never see the whole of Him, as He is far too vast and complex.

If each one of us is able only to grasp a small part of how amazing God is, then we have two options: we can shrink God so that our small bit is all that He is, and thereby create a miniature God, or we can gather with others and share all our little bits of God. It is in community that each of us gets a glimpse of the almighty God. As we each experience God and share that with one another, we start to build a bigger picture. This moves us on to a stage where we have left our own miniature gods and are able to envision a bigger, corporate God, but it still isn't the whole picture.

The Scriptures only ever describe God as being "like" something. The writers have to do this because they can compare Him only to things that He created. We cannot name the building blocks or describe Him in any other way than by using things with which we are familiar but which fall short of describing the Creator of all things. It is as though we lack the language to describe the ultimate source of all life. We are using things that came from Him to describe who and what He is, whereas He is so much more than merely the things He has made.

The image that we hold of God shapes how we relate to Him; it shapes who we think He is and what we think He is capable of. We need a higher, more glorious vision of Jesus and who He is. We need a bigger concept of the Father, a greater wonder at who He is and what He is capable of by His Spirit. As Tozer beautifully puts it, "The heaviest obligation lying upon the Christian church today is to purify and elevate her concept of God."[4]

In this first section we are going to look at how we can "elevate our concept of God" by looking at some things that minimize our view of who God is. We are going to lift our eyes from the miniature gods and look higher than we have looked before. Then, as our eyes look up and our vision improves, we will see the glory of who this magnificent God really is: He's the God of immeasurably greater possibility, majesty, and splendour.

NARROW GOD

I've recently had to start wearing glasses. I've been told I have the vision of someone ten years older than me. Generally I don't have a problem wearing the spectacles but the other day as I was sitting in a meeting with someone, I realized that there was a gentleman in the background skulking and up to no good. I tried to watch him out of the corner of my eye but as he moved around he kept moving just in and out of my vision. My glasses were stopping me from seeing a wider picture. Taking off my glasses, I was able to see more widely than with them. The frames were giving me a narrower view of the sight before me. Sometimes it is as though we are like this with God. Could it be that we need a bigger and more glorious vision of God and without realizing it something has crept in and narrowed our imagination down?

As Paul says in Colossians 1:15, if Jesus is the vision of the invisible God, making this unknowable God known, then maybe in the way we have narrowed our view of God, we have done the same with Jesus.

Think about Jesus. What is the image of Jesus that you are drawn to? All too often, the Jesus that fills our imagination isn't the rebellious Galilean who spoke out against injustice, spoke harshly to the

religious world, and spent time with outcasts. Nor is it the Jesus who died in humiliation and rose again as King of the universe, now reigning in glory on the throne of heaven with angels singing praise and adoration to Him each second that passes. It is entirely possible that we imagine a Jesus significantly less glorious. The Jesus who is our friend and our guide is a valid image, but not the only description of Him we find in the Bible.

In the fashion world over the last few years, a stereotypical picture of Jesus has been found, often on t-shirts or handbags: He has blue eyes and blond hair, and a purple sash with a white tunic. Some people when they think of Jesus will picture this slightly "kitsch" image. Others may still picture the "nice" simple Jesus we met in Sunday school, meek and sanitized for children. The Jesus of our culture is so caricatured that many people no longer know the real Jesus; they know a plastic fake god, a god with little power and little to offer us, not worth spending time thinking about.

I see evidence of this limited image of Jesus when people say to me that they have looked into Christianity but decided it didn't work. I always follow up their comment with the invitation:

"Tell me about the Jesus that didn't work for you..."

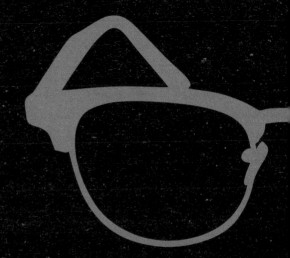

MANY CALL ME RELIGIOUS AND SOME CALL ME DEVOUT
BUT MY PLASTIC JESUS RIDES WITH ME ALL DAY THROUGHOUT.

ATTACHED TO MY DASHBOARD JESUS RIDES WITH ME TO WORK,
HIS HEAD APPEASING MY SIN WITH A SIMPLE NOD AND SHERK.

MY NODDING **PLASTIC JESUS** IS MUCH BETTER THAN THE REAL,
HE ASKS SO LITTLE OF ME AND NEVER DEMANDS THE STEERING WHEEL.

MY JESUS ENSHRINED IN PLASTIC HE'S EVER SO SPOTLESS,
NEVER DOES HE SPOIL MY FUN OR EVEN CALL ME POMPOUS.

NO SALVATION NEEDED WITH THE FAITH THAT JESUS SPINS,
HE SIMPLY SITS THERE GRINNING, BLESSING FROM HIS PLASTIC LIMBS.

STANDING ON MY DASHBOARD JESUS DOESN'T LEAVE THE CAR,
HE CAN'T SEE WHAT I'M DOING WHEN I'VE SINFULLY GONE TOO FAR.

NO NEED FOR BRICKS OR MORTAR TO WORSHIP THIS PLASTIC GOD,
ALL I NEED FROM MY DRIVING SEAT IS TO RETURN HIS RELIGIOUS NOD.

I CRIED TO MY PLASTIC JESUS BUT HE DIDN'T HEAR MY VOICE,
I'M NOT SURE THIS, RELIGION THING, IS MY REAL CHOICE.

MY MARRIAGE IS NOW OVER AND I'M LIVING IN THE RED,
MY PLASTIC SMILING JESUS A TEAR HE DOESN'T SHED.

I DON'T KNOW WHY I BOTHER, MY COMMITMENT SEEMS TOO MUCH,
I GET LITTLE IN RETURN FROM HIM I THINK HE'S OUT OF TOUCH.

I THINK I MIGHT RETURN HIM TO THE SHOP I BOUGHT HIM FROM,
I COULD HAVE BOUGHT A BUDDHA DOLL, ST MARY OR ST JOHN.

Cris Rogers – My Plastic Jesus

Every time people say they have found Jesus to be an empty promise, what they have found isn't the real Jesus but a smaller and less significant version. It is then possible to push them on what they did find. What they are often talking about is immeasurably less than the reality, and often as they describe the Jesus they have rejected I have to agree that what they are talking about is a plastic, cheap version of something so wonderful.

Others carry around in their heads fake gods that have turned them away from a life of faith, but they are content with them because they don't demand much. Countless numbers of people enjoy the lucky-charm god because he asks little of them but helps them when they need it. However, when this god fails them, which he does eventually, they end up throwing the whole package away. All of these are smaller images of the immeasurably bigger true God.

This struggle to engage with the bigger God isn't just about a lack of imagination or the inability of our minds to comprehend the amazing size of God. It is more deliberate than that, and we find its source in the book of Genesis.

The story of Genesis is the story of the devil tricking God's people into seeing Him as something He isn't. Genesis 1 opens with a glorious creation narrative. We see God creating with the sheer power of words. We see His love of creating, making, and sorting. We see His vastness, power, and splendour. The story tells that He creates man and woman and places them in the garden to work with Him, but then the account takes a sad turn. The devil (*Asatan* in Hebrew, meaning deceiver or trickster) shows up and significantly shrinks the imagination of Adam and Eve. The snake approaches the people and convinces them that if they eat the fruit of the tree then they "will be like God, knowing good and evil". The devil claims that God has lied and is using the tree to prevent Adam and Eve from gaining the same power that He has.

"God is lying to you; God is hiding this from you."

To Adam and Eve, God is no longer truth, purity, beauty, and majesty; He's a deceitful, lying, power-hungry and worthless being.

The devil's ploy was to attack God's goodness. If he could shrink Adam and Eve's view of God by calling Him a liar, then he could reduce their attachment to Him, and he's been doing the same ever since. If the devil can convince you that God is a smaller version of Himself, then you will not trust or obey Him because He isn't as powerful as you'd hoped.

CREATED GODS

Paul spoke to the people of Ephesus about precisely this when he tried to tell them that they had created and were selling significantly miniaturized gods. Paul says that "gods made by human hands are no gods at all" (Acts 19:26). These handmade gods surround the people of Ephesus and give them the impression of a god that isn't particularly powerful.

I live in an area that is 65 per cent Muslim. These 65 per cent believe that Allah is the only God and that Jesus is a prophet. The Jesus they speak of and the Jesus I speak of are totally and distinctly different. Same name, different person. Last year we had a huge banner outside our church asking people to answer the question "Jesus is...?".

We invited people to text in who they thought Jesus was. Many responses said a prophet; some said a good moral teacher, and another said the Spanish guy who repaired their car. It's possible to hear the name "Jesus" and for what comes to mind to be significantly smaller and less challenging than the real Jesus.

The challenge is, then, to look at whether the version of Jesus that we as Christians believe in is limited and unchallenging compared to the one found in our Scriptures. As we have seen, it is possible for us to think of Jesus but actually to understand Him as a significantly smaller God than He really is.

LACKING IN SUBSTANCE

Imagine having a plastic figurine called Jesus: you pray to Him, you worship Him, and you ask Him to direct your life. But as long as you worship a plastic version of Jesus rather than the living, breathing God, your heart will only ever focus on something that in name is Jesus but in substance is nothing. C. S. Lewis in *The Screwtape Letters* talks of these small, inferior gods that we set up as being "straw gods". They look like God on the outside but haven't got the substance of Him.

This was something I struggled with when I was younger. As I grew up, my vision of Jesus was a narrow one. I saw Jesus as nothing but a religious figure, like the ones in all the other religions. This changed only when I experienced the might and power of God by His presence.

These reduced images of Jesus and God are like the small clay gods of earlier times. They are dangerous, and need naming, taming, and destroying so that we can begin to see the wonder of the God of immeasurably more. This distorted image of God may start off with a "truth" about God's personality, but then it gets shrunk and limited, becoming an untruth and leaving us with a flimsy caricature of the real thing.

Some of these false theologies come to us from folklore, old wives' tales, and misunderstood ideas, and some from the characters within jokes. But each of these mini gods leads us dangerously to a significantly diluted and enfeebled being. Is the God whom we worship the true and powerful God, or is He a significantly powerless god of our own creation?

Is our God limited in power, limited in location, and limited in what He knows?

Or...

Is our God omnipotent (unlimited in power), omnipresent (unlimited in space and time), and omniscient (unlimited in knowledge)?

We can think we worship one type of God but actually be worshipping the other without even knowing it. We might attend an orthodox church, sing orthodox hymns, and never realize we are worshipping a significantly lesser God.

But how do we know which one we are worshipping? These distortions of who God is can be taken out and looked at, like the idols worshipped thousands of years ago. A few common ones are:

- **The cosy God**, who helps us to feel comforted but never challenges us.

- **The lucky-charm God**, who can be kept in your pocket or on your key ring like a rabbit's foot.

- **The God of moral teaching**, who speaks to His followers through a moralizing whisper in the ear, but what He says is very subjective.

- **The angry God**, whom we work to appease with good behaviour.

- **The old-man God**, who is unaware of how things really are, but we look fondly on Him with a sense of nostalgia.

- **The perfect but absent God**, who can't come near us because He is in danger of being made unclean by our sin.

- **The second-hand God** of "this is what my family believes".

    QUESTION: Which aspects of these gods do you find in your idea of the one true God?

    QUESTION: Are there two or three that maybe merge to create a god that looks like Jesus but is less powerful?

    Often we can all be using the name "Jesus" but what we are really talking about is a less significant version of Him.

    QUESTION: What impact does this have on how you personally need to respond to Jesus?

    QUESTION: Are there any old gods you need to pack away to open yourself up to Jesus?

God is calling His church to look up and see the glory and wonder of who and what He really is. To see the unlimited power He holds, the unlimited space He possesses, and the unlimited knowledge and wisdom He enjoys.

As Jude puts it, "To him who is able to keep you from stumbling and to present you before his glorious presence without fault and with great joy – to the only God our Saviour be glory, majesty, power and authority, through Jesus Christ our Lord before all ages, now and for ever! Amen."[5] Can I hear an Amen?

Jude has glimpsed a vision of God that is expanding his heart, mind, and imagination. He uses the words **"glory"**, **"majesty"**, **"power"**, **"authority"**, **"for ever and ever"**. The vision Jude has of God brings him to kneel before Him in worship. (More about kneeling in a moment...) This vision leads Jude to see God as ever more glorious, magnificent, wonderful, powerful, and splendid. Paul writes in 1 Timothy, "Now to the King eternal, immortal, invisible, the only God, be honour and glory for ever and ever."[6] Paul isn't just stating a fact; he's praising God in adoration. Paul has a higher vision than simply one of a controller of the universe; he sees a King eternal who is immortal, invisible, and unique.

BEND THE KNEE

Paul writes in Ephesians 3:14 that "for this reason I kneel before the Father...".

This section of the Bible was originally written in Greek. The Greek words used here that we translate as "kneel" are actually *kempto* (to bend) and *yovu* (knee). In themselves these two words mean exactly what they translate as, "bend the knee", but their use here is a Semitic idiom. It paints a mental picture of what is happening in the writer's heart. A British idiom would be, for instance, saying "I'm under the weather" when you're feeling ill, or replying "You can say that again!" when something just said is very true.

Bending the knee implies more than just pledging allegiance or making an act of reverence. It's a symbol of devotion, of worship, of making oneself small so as to make the other greater. Assuming a lower position makes the other grander and more lofty.

This idiom is a picture of not only the knee bowing but also the heart. This bowing of the heart is what we would call worship.

We need to back up for a moment and ask the question: Why does Paul write "for this reason" at the start of the verse? Paul says that he bows the knee in worship for "*this reason*". The previous two chapters of the book of Ephesians have painted a picture of who this higher God is.

Paul tells us that God is the one who pours out blessings on His children; they have been adopted into His family, no longer foreigners but children. He says that those of us who were dead are now alive, and in Him we are now built together to become a dwelling place, a tabernacle or a temple for God. And it's because the character of God is revealed through all this that Paul now bends the knee in worship.

God has done what was imaginable.
God has done what was impossible.
God has done what was unfathomable.

So Paul's response is to make God higher and himself lower by bending the knee before Him. There can be a danger that we create a small plastic-figurine version of God, but the God we find in Scripture is a God so awe-inspiring that we can't help but kneel and bow. The question facing us is: Are we interested and willing enough to look up and see Him as exalted and glorious as He really is? Because the cost of doing so is getting down on our knees and worshipping.

A HIGHER GOD AND A GREAT OUTWORKING OF HIS POWER

By being in danger of shrinking God's majesty and glory, we diminish not only Him but also what He is capable of. By believing in a smaller god we end up limiting the way we see God the Father, Son, and Holy Spirit and what He does. We limit Jesus by viewing Him as a "good teacher" or a mere spiritual leader, like Gandhi or some other "good" human leader. Just as our perception of Jesus can be limited, the same is true of the person of the Spirit.

"TRIBES" AND VIEWS OF THE SPIRIT

Generally, our view and opinion of the Holy Spirit is influenced by the teachings of the particular "tribe" of Christianity we come from. Depending on our denomination or church background, we may understand the work of the Holy Spirit differently, and these various ways of understanding don't always fit into neat boxes. It is, however, helpful to be aware and acknowledge that others think differently.

There are some church traditions that focus on a "move of the Spirit", and spend time waiting for the Holy Spirit to speak, as well as seeking spiritual gifts. In these traditions, people also speak of seeing manifestations of the Spirit, which can include people falling, shaking, or speaking in tongues. Miracles of healing are also seen as a part of the Spirit's work. Other churches focus more specifically on the gift of speaking in tongues as a mark that the Spirit is at work. Some churches with this kind of focus will also see the Spirit as coming to bless and bring success, with a particular emphasis on a "prosperity gospel" in which health and financial wealth are part of the Spirit's blessings.

At the other end of the spectrum, there are some churches that tend to avoid speaking about the Holy Spirit, not attributing much to the power of the Spirit today. Other churches will talk about the Holy Spirit as primarily having a role in convicting us of sin and revealing truth in Scripture – making us aware of what needs changing in us and enabling us to effect that change.

In between, there are churches that acknowledge the presence of the Holy Spirit in all their services, but in a low-key way. This can include using incense to help people to visualize the Spirit and a life of prayer, or an awareness of the Spirit being there to strengthen and support us, like a background hum. These churches might see the gift of tongues as an experience found only on the day of Pentecost, rather than in the present.

All of the traditions described here are looking at only part of the picture – peering through a narrow window at just one or two aspects of the Holy Spirit.

We need to view the Spirit from many different angles. As when light is reflected through a gem such as a diamond, and when you turn it the light shines differently, so it is with the person of the Spirit. Each church tradition sees one way of the light reflecting; some churches turn the gem a little more and see several ways in which the light moves. What we need to be doing is turning, turning, and turning the stone to see *all* the different angles and reflections of the Spirit, thus creating a beautiful kaleidoscope of colour.

Immeasurably More: Small-Group Study

QUESTION: What are the mini gods that you see living and breathing in your community? These are the idols or mini versions of Jesus that people create for themselves, without any thought of worshipping them. (You could ask what fake gods surround you...)

QUESTION: Do you think people realize that if they don't worship Jesus as Lord the only alternative is to worship mini gods such as greed, security, worry, and celebrity? Do you think this is obvious to people?

At this point, pray that as we read the passage the Holy Spirit would reveal to us what He is wanting to say through it.

READ: Acts 19:23–41

What jumps out from this passage?

Do you notice something that you haven't seen before or don't understand?

What is God saying to you in this reading?

QUESTION: Why do you think the silversmiths of Ephesus were angry with Paul for challenging their idol-making business?

QUESTION: The whole city was in uproar because Paul had claimed that no idol or mini god was the real God. What do you think Paul was really challenging?

QUESTION: If Paul walked into your village, town, or city, what idols would he challenge?

QUESTION: What idols or mini gods do you cling on to, and do you take offence if they are challenged?

QUESTION: Within the church, we are always in danger of creating a mini version of Jesus, a much less powerful and loving one. Can you pinpoint mini versions of Jesus within your own church family? This may be a version who doesn't heal today, or a much more "religious" Jesus such as is found in stained-glass windows.

PRAY

Pray that your view of God would explode with a higher, closer, deeper, wider, and further vision of Jesus. Pray that where your view of God has been narrowed, by His Holy Spirit it would be expanded, giving you a beautiful kaleidoscopic picture of who He really is.

2 REGAINING WONDER

When I was a young teenager I lived in the north of England. A group of friends and I would pack our bags and go camping in a sacred part of the country called Whitby. It doesn't sound that special, but, trust me, it was. We would camp out in the fields and watch the sun go down while sitting round a campfire baking potatoes. We would often walk the short distance to the cliff and sit with our feet over the edge, dangling down the huge drop to the sea. We would sit there for hours looking out at the North Sea and gazing in wonder at the stars, moon, and planets beyond, and asking, "How could you *not* believe in a God when you see all this?"

Does anyone ever go to a place of great beauty to boost their own self-esteem? We don't come away from beautiful views and announce how great *we* are. If you have ever been to a place such as the Grand Canyon or seen the Aurora Borealis, you can't help but be aware of that innate desire to acknowledge something greater than ourselves.

What makes people drive miles or fly halfway round the world to see something they haven't yet seen with their own eyes? We do it because of the desire for wonder. To see something that will leave us breathless at its beauty.

When we sit on a cliff edge looking out at the magnificence of the cosmos, our soul doesn't cry out "Give me a mirror". We sit there with no trace of self-awareness. We don't notice our needs, or even our breathing. The reason for this is very simple: we were *made to esteem something bigger than ourselves.*

We were made to worship God.

The trouble is, our imagination has shrunk until we just can't envisage something as spectacular as God, so we have shrivelled down our own creativity.

The Aurora Borealis

During a lecture, author and former bishop Tom Wright once said:

> *I have debated in public in America with [those] who refuse to believe in the bodily resurrection and again and again the bottom line is when they say, "I just can't imagine that." And the answer is, smarten up your imagination! And the way to do that, is not to beat them over the head with dogma, but so to create a world of mystery and beauty and possibility... there are some pieces of music which when you come out of them it is much easier to say I believe in the Father and the Son and the Holy Spirit than when you went in."*[1]

As Wright says, people don't need beating over the head with theology but they do need us to create the kind of world where people's sense of wonder, mystery, and endless possibility widens their view rather than shrivels and shrinks it. We describe some people as narrow-minded and others as open-minded. Often, these narrow and wide minds exist because someone has either a closed or an open sense of wonder. When we have a closed sense of wonder we can't see how things could be any different; we can't see any other possibilities. Maybe you know people like this, or maybe you yourself identify with this. People like this can be cynical, pessimistic, sceptical, and distrustful. But those people who have an open sense of wonder can see the endless possibilities each day holds. They see beauty where others often see desolation; they see creativity, awe, and colour where others see monotone.

Someone with an open sense of wonder sees God in a multitude of places.

I think this is one reason we are told to come to Jesus as little children. Children don't put things into boxes like adults do. My son Isaac has a low fear level. We recently went on holiday and Isaac was keen to learn to skateboard. We bought him a new deck and headed out each night for me to show him how to skate. I had learned to skate as a young adult and I was full of fear. Fear of falling off, fear of getting it wrong, and fear of looking silly. Isaac had no such fear and soon he was flying down hills at great speed. He fell off one night, grazing his face, arm, and knees. The very next day he was back out on the deck again skating. Children are often willing to have a go and risk falling over and bouncing back up. It's been my experience that we adults have a much more developed awareness of how we could get hurt if we fall, and thus end up being far more fearful.

Children are open to what a new day holds. A child looks at a box of Lego and instead of random pieces they see bricks that hold potential as they play their part in a bigger whole. Children looking at Lego don't see what it "isn't" but what it could "become". They see how each brick could create a giant tower, a spacecraft, a house, a plane, a horse stable, a church, a clock, a train, a table, or even a tree. They see the endless possibilities.

Jesus tells His disciples to become like a child again; to regain their wide-eyed sense of wonder at the world.

QUESTION: What has widened your sense of wonder in the past? What has opened your eyes to God's glory in creation?

QUESTION: What things have narrowed your sense of wonder? What events in your life have left your imagination shrivelled?

SHUFFLING ALONG

Paul understood this sense of childlike wonder. He writes in Colossians 3:2 (MSG): "Don't shuffle along, eyes to the ground, absorbed with the things right in front of you. Look up, and be alert to what is going on around Christ – that's where the action is. See things from *his* perspective."

Paul realized our tendency to shuffle along. When we do this we lose wonder, but when we look up we see the world opening up. Children are like this when they walk into a toy shop; they walk in with head high and eyes jumping from one wondrous sight to another.

Next time you are sitting on a bus or a park bench, watch the people around you. You will see that many people are walking along with their heads down, looking at the ground. It is particularly prevalent in London, where many people just want to be left alone. Some even have that "don't bother me" face. Bus stops are full of people clicking on their little electronic devices. "I'm reading the news," they say, but what they are really doing is locking themselves away. They are absorbed by themselves and their own thoughts.

I was walking in a busy tube station the other day and found myself darting around tube users who were rushing along the tunnels with their eyes glued to their mobile phones. They were so heedless of the other tube users that they just assumed they would move aside for them.

If we're living our life plugged into the worlds within our mobile devices, we shouldn't be surprised when we struggle to find wonder in a big, beautiful, expansive, and dynamic God.

We allow the wonder and amazement of God to sit quietly on a shelf like an expensive vase, while a stream of family, work, and other concerns carries us on relentlessly from day to day. To stop and wonder about God and His goodness, glory, and majesty, and look up from the daily grind to enjoy His creation, should become the priority of our life and not a mere afterthought.

Sometimes we find we have lost our sense of the miracle of life and the beauty of creation. Tozer writes that "[t]his world, after all our science and sciences, is still a miracle; wonderful, inscrutable, magical and more, to whosoever will think of it... Secularism, materialism, and the intrusive presence of things have put out the light in our souls and turned us into a generation of zombies. We cover our deep ignorance with words, but we are ashamed to wonder, we are afraid to whisper 'mystery'."[2]

Tozer is arguing that the things around us have turned us into a "generation of zombies" unable to wonder at the mystery and majesty of God. If we look at ourselves honestly before God, we may recognize times when we have succumbed to this; times when we have allowed the wonder in us to die, and when we shuffle around engrossed in the created instead of raising our eyes to the Creator.

Isaiah was a man steeped in wonder. It oozed out of him onto the pages of his book. In chapter 40 he asks the age-old question of who is this God that we worship, and God replies:

"To whom will you compare me?
Or who is my equal?" says the Holy One.
Lift up your eyes and look to the heavens:
Who created all these?
He who brings out the starry host one by one
and calls forth each of them by name.
Because of his great power and mighty strength,
not one of them is missing.

Why do you complain, Jacob?
Why do you say, Israel,
"My way is hidden from the Lord;
my cause is disregarded by my God"?
Do you not know?
Have you not heard?
The Lord is the everlasting God,
the Creator of the ends of the earth.
He will not grow tired or weary,
and his understanding no one can fathom.
He gives strength to the weary
and increases the power of the weak.
Even youths grow tired and weary,
and young men stumble and fall;
but those who hope in the Lord
will renew their strength.
They will soar on wings like eagles;
they will run and not grow weary,
they will walk and not be faint.
Isaiah 40:25–31

Isaiah stands back with wonder, gazing at a God whom he struggles to put words to; a God who is higher, closer, deeper, wider, and further than he can comprehend.

Isaiah is trying, in the words of Tozer, to turn our lights back on. He is directing our gaze to a point well beyond ourselves and crying out, "Lift up your eyes and look to the heavens; look beyond your cliff edge, to the one who created these stars." He isn't pointing to yet another clay god, fake and flimsy, but to the majestic star originator, the one who has made them all.

To ensure that we don't misinterpret this work as simply the act of a Creator God setting the world in motion, like a ticking clock, Isaiah makes it very clear that this God is intimately involved. The God who names the stars also renews the weary with strength. In pointing outwards to the infinite universe Isaiah is at the same time reminding us that this God is also the one who meets with us in the littleness of our own lives.

This God is active; He is present, and He is with us.

Take a moment to breathe that in. Your God is active, present, and with you.

This is a confounding statement!

The more I come to realize that God, the Creator of the universe, is active and present for me, the more I accept that my response needs to be worship and bowing the knee. The God whom we worship is beyond anything we could imagine in size and scope and yet is intimately involved with our lives. The glorious, almighty, and powerful God is attentive to and active for us, not as a slave to our needs but as a friend who just also happens to be our King.

NAMING STARS

Let's just keep breathing this in for a little while longer...

Neil Armstrong, the first man on the moon, once said to *Time* magazine, "I remember on the trip home on Apollo 11 it suddenly struck me that that tiny pea, pretty and blue, was the earth. I put up my thumb and shut one eye, and my thumb blotted out the planet earth. I didn't feel like a giant. I felt very, very small."[3]

For Armstrong, the experience of doing something that nobody on earth had ever done before didn't make him feel "big" and important. Engaging with the enormity of the universe and realizing how small the earth and especially we are in comparison made him feel exceedingly small. Most of the time we move around our world convinced of our own importance, but as we begin to think about the vast universe and try to imagine the edges of it, we find ourselves shrinking. As we do so, our concept of God grows, and as a consequence our awe at Him and His abilities also grows.

BEHOLD A UNIVERSE SO IMMENSE THAT I AM LOST IN IT. I NO LONGER KNOW WHERE I AM. I AM JUST NOTHING AT ALL. OUR WORLD IS TERRIFYING IN ITS INSIGNIFICANCE.

BERNARD LE BOVIER DE FONTENELLE (1657–1757)

This universe that we live in is indeed amazing. When we sit on that cliff edge, with an *unaided eye*, in dark skies, we can count a few thousand stars. If we were to sit and look with perfect eyesight during a perfect dark night, between the northern and southern hemispheres we would be able to see around 9,000 stars.

We are told that there are somewhere around 100 billion galaxies in the known universe and that's just the bit we know about; there is so much more that we can't yet see. It's as though we have turned the light on in one corner of a room but the room is so big we can't see the other corners. Each of these galaxies has approximately 100 billion stars.

Which means that there are 100 billion galaxies containing 100 billion stars.

Yet the Bible says that God calls each star by name.[4]

Things like that make me wonder whether there really are that many names, or whether He used some twice. It makes naming the animals seem an almost incidental task. Do you think He did it over a few long weekends, or did He have angelic help?

We have delusions of grandeur. We think we are more powerful than we are, more significant than the reality is. We might think we are the most powerful ruler or emperor of all time, but as we look at the night sky we are reminded of one thing: we aren't as big as we think we are.

We are significantly smaller.

As Hermann Hagedorn puts it...

> We are such little men when the
> stars come out,
> So small under the open maw of the night,
> That we must shout and pound the table
> and drive wild,
> And gather dollars and madly dance
> and drink deep,
> And send the great birds flying,
> and drop death.
> When the stars come out we are
> such little men
> That we must arm ourselves in glare
> and thunder,
> Or cave in on our own dry littleness.[5]

SO WHAT?

So He's able to name stars; can't we all do that now on www.name-a-star.com?

Rather than acknowledging God's sovereignty over all things, we patronize Him by offering Him a look-in at certain parts of our life. God has no equals, God is supreme, and nothing is greater or more valuable than He is. As we look at the night sky we become sadly aware of not being as powerful as we like to think we are. In the same way, as we gaze on God and His splendour, we get this sinking feeling.

We don't really control anything, do we?!

When we think God has finished, He reminds us He has immeasurably more; when we think He's run out of steam He has immeasurably more; when we believe that God's done with miracles He tells us He has immeasurably more.

GOD IN A BOX

Most of us in the church are aware that we are not the zombies that Tozer talks about; we are aware of God and we are engaged with Him, but all too often our sense of wonder has begun to dull. It's not that we have lost our faith completely, but a familiarity has crept in that begins to breed complacency, and even contempt. In losing that sense of wonder, awe, and splendour, we are also diluting God's majesty. In other words, we have tamed the untameable in our minds. Let's make this very clear for a moment: God is simply who God is, and regardless of what we think or say about Him He is still the ultimate reality. God is the great "I Am" even if we choose not to see it. No matter what we think or say, He is still supreme wonder and glory.

The truth is, however, that by losing the wonder we have limited God; we've separated Him from His power and we have created a little black holy "God box" to put Him in. It is usually called Sunday, and we come and peer into this box when we have time. By putting

God in this box we have limited His unlimitedness. We've capped His furious, raging love and created a pet who loves us a little. We have dangerously abandoned a powerful, grand, and glorious perception of God and replaced it with something cheap and mean. This thing we have diluted God down into is now so little that we can simply ignore it.

We compartmentalize God in our minds and turn Him into something containable and controllable. Essentially, we aim to manage God and become the god of God.

It's either this or we behave as if He is deluded in thinking He has any power.

So we drop in at church, arriving late, smile at a friend we've not seen in a while, and maybe lean over to a neighbour in our row and make a comment about the pastor's shirt. We act as if it is totally commonplace to meet this epic, expansive, powerful God. The danger is that we have trivialized this enigmatic, mysterious, puzzling, unfathomable, and inexplicable presence into something we would see in a museum.

A TYPICAL INVITATION TO GOD

IT'S RATHER TONGUE IN CHEEK, BUT DO READ THIS LETTER TO GOD. IT'S CHEEKY BUT ALSO SADLY OFTEN PERTINENT. IT LEAVES ME WONDERING HOW OFTEN I HAVE BEHAVED IN THIS WAY WITH GOD IN MAKING SURE I CAN CONTROL OUR NEAT AND TIDY CHURCH GATHERINGS.

Dear God,

We the members of the church called (insert name) will be having our regular weekly meeting this coming Sunday.

We cordially invite You to attend this meeting, providing You kindly consider the following:

From 10:00 – 10:30 we will be singing praises to You and your Son. Perhaps the Holy Spirit too. So during this time please join in, but do not interrupt the programme so lovingly prepared by our worship team.

From 10:30 – 10:40 we will be collecting our gift which we offer to You. (It's really the minister's salary, though).

From 10:40 – 11:15 we will be listening to the well-prepared sermon our pastor will deliver this week, so please sit quietly and listen to what he has worked so hard to offer us.

From 11:20 – 11:35 we will probably be offering some more singing, and perhaps silent prayer.

From 11:40 – 11:50 (?) we will possibly have to listen to some important announcements to do with church activities or programmes.

From 11:55 – 12:15 or so, we will be having coffee and cookies; please feel free to join us during this time of fellowship.

You are welcome to make Your Presence known any time during this service providing You follow our carefully laid out agenda.

Kindly RSVP

Don't be surprised if He declines your invitation.

www.simply-jesus-christ.com/gpage6.html

GOD DOES NOT LIVE IN OUR RELIGIOUS BOXES

We need to think more highly of God, remembering that He is incomprehensible, rather than conceiving Him in our minds in our own image, and limiting His beauty to our own crude understanding.

If God has made us in his image, we have returned him the favour.[6]

God does not live in boxes. He helped the Jewish people in the exodus story by giving them the ark of the covenant, but He didn't need a box to live in. The golden chest they made was to act as a focal point for them, but we have created boxes for God to live in.

Some of these boxes have names...

- Religion
- This is how God works
- This is how God thinks of me
- This group of people aren't welcome
- Not for the irreligious
- Sacred
- Out of date

Over time, we might come to realize that God is bigger than we imagined in the first place, but all too often we merely take Him out of one box and pop Him into a larger one.

God should get more from us on Sunday mornings than He does. I don't want to blaspheme God in my sermons by making Him smaller than He is, but I want to share one thing every Sunday: the supremacy of God over all things. I don't want to shrink God to fit my preconceived ideas; *I* want to shrink so that He will become bigger in my view. God should get far more from us in our worship. We should be getting a crick in our neck because we are looking higher and higher in wonder at our amazing Creator.

God is bigger than our imagination can ever cope with.

If we are going to speak about stars and the cosmos, then we might find it helpful to learn from Albert Einstein. Charles Misner, a scientific relativity theorist of the twentieth century, once wrote this of him:

> *I do see the design of the universe as essentially a religious question – that is, one should have some kind of respect and awe for the whole business. It is very magnificent and should not be taken for granted. In fact, I believe that is why Albert Einstein had so little use for organized religion – although he strikes me as a very religious man. Einstein must have looked at what the preachers said about God and felt they were blaspheming. He had seen much more majesty than they had ever imagined, and they were just not talking about the real thing.*[7]

We need to be careful that we don't miss the "real thing" by limiting and minimizing our image of God. We need to reclaim that wonder and awe at our amazing God, who is bigger than we could ever imagine.

We have to let go of our disappointingly limited taster of what is really possible and accept that God is offering us immeasurably more.

Immeasurably More: Small-Group Study

QUESTION: Someone with an open sense of wonder sees God in all kinds of places, but some people simply can't see God at work around them. What things do you think feed into this inability to see God? Some ideas could include past hurt, feeling let down by God, or disappointments.

QUESTION: What has caused your sense of wonder to fade away? How honest can you be?

At this point, pray that as we read the passage the Holy Spirit would reveal to us what He is wanting to say through it.

READ: Colossians 3:1–4

What jumps out from this passage?

Do you notice something you haven't seen before or don't understand?

What is God saying to you in this reading?

Now read the passage in *The Message* translation.

Colossians 3:2: "Don't shuffle along, eyes to the ground, absorbed with the things right in front of you. Look up, and be alert to what is going on around Christ – that's where the action is. See things from *his* perspective."

QUESTION: "Shuffling along": do you think this is what we do? Are we "shufflers"?

QUESTION: God is bigger than our imagination can comprehend, so what reasons do you think there are for our desire to contain God and box Him in?

QUESTION: Religion can be understood as our way of trying to get closer to God. What does the passage say about what has happened and how we now relate to God? Is it through our striving (religious behaviour) or through what He has done?

QUESTION: In the reading, we are told to set our hearts on things above. What are these things?

QUESTION: Rather than giving ourselves to a relationship with Jesus, we are always in danger of giving ourselves over to "religion" and religious practices. The passage says that our life appears when we *give* our life to Jesus. Faith in Jesus is about life, not death. Are you able to see any instances where you might have placed religion above Jesus?

QUESTION: Gaining life through Jesus is the central idea of Christianity. How much does this surprise you? Does it make you excited and help to deepen your wonder and amazement at God?

PRAY

Pray that you might not miss the "real thing" by looking too hard at religion or the idea of God. Where might you have been disappointed by faith and Jesus up to this point? Hand this to God and pray that He would help you regain your sense of wonder at who He is and what He is able to do.

3 TOO FAMILIAR?

A third danger in our relationship with God is that we can become too familiar with Him. It is not merely that we lose our sense of wonder, but that we may end up perceiving Him as our "pal", on an equal footing with us. We may have gone too far and lost any sense of awe at who He is: as the modern quip goes, we can tend to regard Him as "All-Matey" rather than "Almighty". For us to be truly in awe of this Supreme Being, we need to have a correct understanding of how small we are in comparison to Him. Having a higher and more glorious vision of God will enable us to respond appropriately and express the truth of Him in worship.

Tozer recognized that our bowing of the knee is inextricably linked to our view of God:

> Worship, I say, rises or falls with our concept of God; that is why I do not believe in these half-converted cowboys who call God the Man Upstairs. I do not think they worship at all because their concept of God is unworthy of God and unworthy of them. And if there is one terrible disease in the Church of Christ, it is that we do not see God as great as He is. We're too familiar with God.[1]

This is not to undermine the intimacy and closeness that we may experience in worship or prayer, particularly with Jesus, whom many of us might consider our closest friend. It's in Jesus that the all-powerful Creator becomes known also as the personal friend. But it is about ensuring that that is not the only way we have of relating to God. It is certainly not a way of relating that we find particularly often in the Bible.

We need to shrink so that He might grow. We need to learn not to see ourselves as being on a level with God.

This is nothing new. It's not a modern problem that we have stumbled across. John the Baptist was also aware that we need to shrink so that Jesus can grow. In John 3, John announces:

> *He must become greater; I must become less. The one who comes from above is above all; the one who is from the earth belongs to the earth, and speaks as one from the earth. The one who comes from heaven is above all.*
>
> John 3:30–31 (MSG)

The believers in the early church understood that the nearer they drew to the God of immeasurably more, the more profoundly they became aware of their own lowliness and limitations. As they knelt lower, God became bigger.

Aristides, an Athenian philosopher, wrote in AD 137 to the Emperor of Rome about the behaviour of the early Christians. In the midst of quite a telling statement about the church, he writes that "[t]hey speak gently to those who oppress them, and in this way, they make their enemies their friends. It has become their passion to do good to their enemies. They live in the awareness of their own smallness."

The correct responses to all that God says – in the pages of His book, by the revelation of His Spirit, and through the splendour of His creation – are awe and reverence. Our response to the greatness of God should be to fall on our knees.

They lived in the awareness of their own smallness...

AWE, WONDER, AND FEAR

I grew up with a love of cricket. It didn't last long, but nevertheless for a time I loved it. My joy in the sport ended rather abruptly when I knocked out another child's front tooth. Over the last year I have started to re-engage with it – not for myself but for my nine-year-old son, Isaac, who, it turns out, is really good at cricket. We went out as a family for an afternoon at the Oval Cricket Club and watched a fantastic game. Isaac was in awe of one particular batsman who stayed in for the whole game. He didn't get bowled out. It was truly spectacular.

At the end of the game Isaac ran off to get this player's autograph. Isaac stood in silent awe of this superstar as he walked past and signed his programme.

Isaac's jaw dropped in awe.

Have we become so familiar with God that we have lost this sense of jaw-dropping awe as we look at Him?

Some years ago I was learning to surf, and the waves were getting heavier and stronger by the moment. I was out on my own and the waves came one after the other, and I ended up under the water trying to grab a breath before the next one battered me under again.

It wasn't long before I was back out on the stormy waters trying to find that perfect wave and lift myself up to ride it back to the beach. Sadly, the ocean was just too powerful and strong for me, and it knocked me clean off the board. As I went under, the board hit the front of my head and the next wave knocked all the breath out of me. I ended up being dragged up the beach by this wave, gasping and beaten. In my soggy wetsuit I must have looked like a stranded whale.

That's when I discovered the power of the ocean, and *I was in awe*.

As humans on planet earth, we often drop our jaws at things natural: sunsets and sunrises, beautiful views, and starry nights. We have mastered the art of worshipping without even knowing it. We talk about our experiences with our friends. We are in awe of beauty, art, creativity, the rousing sound of an orchestra, or the misty beauty of a cold winter's day.

But let's imagine for a moment that we came physically face to face with the real God. I think we'd freak out... a lot...

...and I would argue that the Bible agrees.

There is this wonderful moment in the story of Daniel when we are told that King Belshazzar is having a wild party, with noblemen drinking heavily. During this gathering a human hand appears and a finger starts to write on the plaster of the wall.

Just to explain, the phrase "finger of God" is used only a few times in the Bible. The finger of God brings the plagues in Exodus 8. In Exodus 31 we are told that the covenant law is inscribed on the stone tablets by the "finger of God". In Psalm 8 we are told that the moon and the stars are "the work of [God's] fingers". Jesus casts out demons in Luke 11 with the "finger of God", and writes freedom on the ground for a prostitute with His "finger".

The finger of God thus came to indicate God's rule, power, judgment, and authority as well as to signify a moment at which God is changing the direction of things for His people.

In Daniel 5:5–6 we are told that the finger of God appears and writes on the plaster of the wall.

> *The king watched the hand as it wrote. His face turned pale and he was so frightened that his legs became weak and his knees were knocking.*

Obviously, seeing a free-floating hand inscribing your doom on the wall is enough to make anyone's knees knock. But look at it like this: King Belshazzar didn't need to see the whole of God to find his knees knocking and his legs giving way. When we see *anything* of God our knees should give way, not because it is meant to be scary but because we are *supposed to* be bowing before Him.

THE PRIESTS OF BAAL

The Bible is full of stories of people falling on their knees or even faces in awe. The shepherds and astrologers all do it when they see the baby Jesus. In 2 Chronicles 5, we are told that God Himself showed up at the Temple, and it says that the priests who were working there that day were so transfixed that they couldn't perform their priestly duties. People see God's "immeasurably more" and it leaves them on their knees, torn apart by fear and falling to the ground as though dead.

In 1 Kings 18 we have this wonderful story of Elijah the prophet. He has found himself in a "god war" with a bunch of priests from the temple of Baal. Well, it was more than a bunch; we are told that there were 450 of them, to be precise. This group of people had been wavering for some time over whether they would worship the god Baal or the God YHVH. YHVH (or Yahweh, as we pronounce it) was the name of the Jewish God that was given to Moses at the burning bush. Elijah is at his wits' end with them and decides that a "god-off" is needed. We are all now familiar with the concept of a "bake-off". This would have been a similar process, only with the winner being declared the one true God.

It is agreed that two bulls will be sacrificed for the event and that each side will pray to their god to set fire to the prepared offering, placed on a stack of wood. Elijah announces that the priests of Baal can go first and call on the name of their god, and then he will call on the name of his God. The one who answers by fire, Elijah states, is God.

The god-off is launched and the priests of Baal go first. The story goes that they call on the name of Baal from early morning until noon. "Baal, answer us!" they shout. But there is no response; no one answers. They dance around the altar they have made, with cries and prayers. The priests end up cutting themselves to try to get Baal's attention, and Elijah tells them to make more of an effort and shout more loudly. Elijah isn't the quiet type, and he ends up goading the priests. At one point he asks them whether their god has gone to the toilet and therefore can't hear them. (By the way, this isn't a good example of an interfaith event. Rule one of an interfaith event is: never shout, "Has your god gone to the loo?")

Then comes the moment for Elijah to step forward. In a moment of cockiness he tells the priests of Baal to drench the wood of the sacrifice, to make the task harder. In fact, he does this three times to make sure it really is soaked. Elijah prays and then the fire of the Lord falls and burns up the bull, the wood, the stones, and the soil – and it even licks up the water in the trench. When all the people see what has happened they fall prostrate and cry, "YHVH – He is God! YHVH – He is God!"

NO ONE STANDS BEFORE GOD

It doesn't matter who you are when you experience the power of the God of immeasurably more; we all fall in awe, our knees knock, and our backs give way.

It's not just the jaw-dropping stuff of the Old Testament that has people falling to their knees. There are moments in the Gospels when people hear Jesus speak and they step back in wonder. In John 18 we are told that, at the time of Jesus' arrest, the powerful Roman guards come to find Him, ready for a fight. They know what kind of person Jesus is. We often think of Jesus as the blue-eyed and blond-haired figure of Western paintings, but they see Him as a dangerous political maverick bent on revolution. Knowing His real power, Pilate has sent an entire detachment to arrest Him in public. Fully aware of what is going on, Jesus asks them, "Who are you looking for?" and they say, "Jesus." And Jesus replies, "I am He." It's at this point that the true power and authority of Jesus is revealed. In the passage, we are told that at that moment the entire detachment of trained, armed Roman officers "drew back and fell to the ground".

This phrase, "fell to the ground", is exactly the same as the one used in connection with the astrologers who bowed before the baby at the nativity. Jesus barely moves and says only a few words, but those words have such power that an entire military garrison involuntarily hits the ground.

No one stands before God.

No one.

There comes a time when you come face to face with something so gorgeous, so powerful, so fearsome in its supremacy that you simply fall down. This is what happens when God comes near.

LIKE LITTLE CHILDREN

> Earth's crammed with Heaven,
> And every common bush aflame with God;
> But only he who sees, takes off his shoes,
> The rest sit round it and pluck blackberries.
>
> **Elizabeth Barrett Browning,** *Aurora Leigh*

Realizing the wonder of God needs to move us to a place of awe and not a place of fear. Some of us will start to open our eyes to this vast, expansive "immeasurably more" God and be fearful. But that's not what God is looking for. He wants us to be like little children, thrilled and full of awe and wonder.

When my son was just under two years old, he was taken to some botanical gardens for the day. In the centre of the gardens was a large cage of beautiful finches. Isaac stood looking up at the cage, silent and still. He wasn't (and isn't) a silent and still child. He loves to move, comment, and understand. Yet Isaac stood in silence, watching with wide eyes these birds fluttering around the cage. You could see the look on his face of "Do I need to learn to do that too?", panicking that he too would need to learn to fly. The sight of those small finches in the cage had moved Isaac to stand still, in silent amazement and reverence.

Awe isn't something we learn or can even really read about. It's something we experience when we look up and see something amazing.

Awe is what you feel when you're a child and see a cage of little finches for the first time.

Awe is what you sense when you stand back on the beach and look round at the waves, knowing they beat you.

Awe is inspired, not taught, by an elder.

Awe comes with a surprise.

Awe involves being filled with curiosity and inquisitiveness.

The psalmist understood this sense of wonder when he wrote: "Taste and see that the Lord is good" (Psalm 34:8). Tasting and seeing are primary senses: taste is used to capture something; it's a sense that leaves us wanting more of something good.

We say that something is "moreish", and this sense of wanting more comes because the taste of it has left us with a degree of awe and wonder. It's a flavour we just have to have more of. We don't taste something good and think, "I daren't have more of that because it's too good."

Rob Bell describes what the psalmist is speaking of in this way: "Tasting is about our flesh and blood encounters with the Divine, taste is about our awareness that God is as close as your breath."[2]

Tasting is about experiencing the wonder of who our God is and what our God has for us. Tasting is about allowing ourselves the moment to experience what this God has for us. Tasting is about looking up, disconnecting from our mobile phone, and being open to experiencing this God of more.

Tasting is about stopping shuffling along, and expecting to sense the awe around us all the time.

Tasting is about saying yes to all the God of more has in store for us.

Tasting is about looking higher than we have before and getting a crick in our neck because what we now see is leaving us with a wide-eyed sense of wonder and awe.

Just last night I looked up and saw the full moon. It was big and bright and awe-inspiring. I found myself looking higher and harder than I had done before. It was as though I was seeing the moon for the very first time, although I have obviously seen it many, many times before.

The invitation of the God of more is to look up higher in awe, see Him for what He really is, and wonder what majestic new thing He is going to do today.

A–Z ACTIVITY

There are many words we could use to describe God: indescribable, magnificent, glorious, mighty, strong, powerful, gracious... Take this list of letters from the alphabet and write a word to describe God next to it. Try to find an adjective (a describing word) that applies to God for each of the letters. Once you have done this, read the list out loud as an act of worship. As you do so, can you feel your sense of awe grow in your belly? As you read the list out, you should find that your sense of awe expands within you like a balloon.

GOD, YOU ARE...

A.

B.

C.

D.

E.

F.

G.

H.

I.

J.

K.

L.

M.

N.

O.

P.

Q.

R.

S.

T.

U.

V.

W.

X.

Y.

Z.

AMEN.

Immeasurably More: Small-Group Study

QUESTION: Do you think that a Christian's apathy or lack of passion could be because they have become too familiar with God?

QUESTION: How long have you had a faith in Jesus? Over time, do you think you can become complacent as you learn more?

At this point, pray that as we read the passage the Holy Spirit would reveal to us what He is wanting to say through it.

READ: John 3:22–36

What jumps out from this passage?

Do you notice something you haven't seen before or don't understand?

What is God saying to you in this reading?

QUESTION: John says that he must become less and Jesus greater. Do you think this was hard for John to say? Do you think there was something in him that would have loved to become known, celebrated, and raised up?

QUESTION: The believers of the early church understood that the nearer they drew to the God of immeasurably more, the more they became aware of their own smallness. As they knelt lower, God became bigger. Do you think this is true today?

QUESTION: John says that Jesus gives the Spirit without limit. What do you think is the link between being given the Spirit without limit and getting on our knees and making ourselves small?

QUESTION: John says that the one from above is above all. Where in our churches do you think we might have tried to make "the church" or our activities greater than God? Why do you think this is?

QUESTION: What is holding you back from making yourself small and God greater in your mind, heart, and life?

QUESTION: John ultimately died for his faith in Jesus. We don't face the danger of death, which means our faith isn't as costly. But what will we need to sacrifice to make Jesus greater in our lives?

PRAY

Our prayer must be for immeasurably less of us, and immeasurably more of Him:

Be here, fully alive in the company of your creator,
Be quiet, fully resting in His peace,
Be still, fully released to the simplicity of waiting,
Be ready, fully aware of the power that is His.
We come, offering ourselves once again to His presence,
We kneel, offering our bodies in response to His rule,
We pause, offering our time to Him who designed it,
We focus, offering our thoughts to His wisdom.

Amen.[3]

IN THE CHRISTIAN LIFE YOU ARE NOT USUALLY LOOKING AT HIM. HE IS ALWAYS ACTING THROUGH YOU. IF YOU THINK OF THE FATHER AS SOMETHING "OUT THERE," IN FRONT OF YOU, AND OF THE SON AS SOMEONE STANDING AT YOUR SIDE, HELPING YOU TO PRAY, TRYING TO TURN YOU INTO ANOTHER SON, THEN YOU HAVE TO THINK OF THE THIRD PERSON AS SOMETHING INSIDE YOU, OR BEHIND YOU.

C. S. Lewis, *Mere Christianity*

A Closer Story
A real story about a person called Ben

My mum was diagnosed with breast cancer when I was thirteen years old. I didn't know it at the time, but the doctors gave her only six weeks to live. Back then I just knew I was very frightened at the prospect of my mum having cancer and possibly dying. My parents shielded me from most of what happened the first time she had chemotherapy, but seeing Mum lose her hair and spend so much time sleeping was hard. I'd always prayed with Dad before bed and we persevered; even though things were tough I still thought God was there, just far away.

After about a year and a half Mum got the all-clear, but then when I was fifteen it came back. By this time I was at boarding school, and the morning after the diagnosis I met with an older friend to pray. I asked in my mind: **"I wonder what God would say if He were here now?"** Almost immediately these words came into my mind out of nowhere: "I am here; I love you; I have a plan." It was such a powerful experience that when I left my friend I literally skipped down the road, full of joy that God had the whole situation in His hands.

Over the next eight years there were more "all-clears" and, painfully, more diagnoses. When I was twenty-one I was studying at university and would go to a Salvation Army house of prayer to worship, singing hymns and worship songs on my own and with friends. When Mum had another diagnosis that year I was determined to keep worshipping and believing that God was good. I still remember those days as a time when I knew God's presence most closely. Although He didn't speak a lot and the situation was as confusing as ever, He was so close that I used to weep tears of joy while singing.

In March 2014 I was coming back from a meeting at work. Straight after the meeting I'd had a call from my dad saying that Mum was deteriorating, and this time we knew it was terminal. As I walked home I passed a small child and his father in the street. The child was walking away from his dad towards a shop window and his dad warned him, "Hold my hand tight. No, you're not holding on tight." The Holy Spirit suddenly pressed the words into my mind: "Are you holding on tight? Hold on tight." In the following four months Mum's health got a lot worse and life was more difficult than ever, but God drew closer and closer.

In the last weeks of her life, God spoke to me countless times through Scripture: text messages from friends pointed me to passages that I studied, which then led me to other passages. On the morning Mum passed away God showed me Isaiah 43:1–3. In the days that followed, a number of others felt that this same passage was for us as a family and were also led to these verses when they prayed for my family.

About a week and a half later I was walking into work and felt the gloom of grief hanging over me. I opened a prayer app on my phone and read the verse: "Though you have made me see troubles, many and bitter, you will restore my life again; from the depths of the earth you will again bring me up" (Psalm 71:20). God was still close and I know He always will be. And yet the closer I find Him to be, the more convinced I am that I still don't know quite how close He really is. But I can't wait to find out.

MOVEMENT TWO
CLOSER

FOR THIS REASON I KNEEL BEFORE THE FATHER, FROM WHOM EVERY FAMILY IN HEAVEN AND ON EARTH DERIVES ITS NAME. I PRAY THAT OUT OF HIS GLORIOUS RICHES HE MAY **STRENGTHEN** YOU WITH **POWER** THROUGH HIS SPIRIT IN YOUR **INNER BEING**, SO THAT CHRIST MAY DWELL IN YOUR HEARTS THROUGH **FAITH**.

Ephesians 3:14–17

Our second movement is "Closer". In seeing God as majestic and marvellous, we can lose the sense of His closeness and presence. In this movement we will come to see that the higher God becomes, the closer He is in Jesus. In the first section, we are going to look at how we have sanitized this powerful God and created "religion", which is only the dressing for the second area we will look at, which is the close relationship we then have with Jesus. We will end by asking how close God really is, and finding that He is as close as lifting a finger.

1 DOES MY RELIGION LOOK BIG IN THIS?

THE PROBLEM

The apostle Paul really loved putting sporting references in his letters. He speaks of gladiator fights, wrestling, climbing, weightlifting, and running. One of the strongest images in his letters is when he compares faith and life to a race. If Paul was right and the life of faith is a race, many of us reach the halfway point and aren't too sure if we can make the finishing line; it just seems so hard and we are so tired.

When the race gets hard and we feel we are far from the finishing line, all too often we find it easier to slip into the ritual and the routine of religion rather than to move closer to and receive more from God. A relationship with a living being needs attention to maintain and sustain it. The church "seems to start up all right and runs a few yards, and then it breaks down. They are trying to run it on the wrong juice."[1] We have taken what is *the* powerful and life-changing message and have carefully sanitized it. Made it easier and more palatable.

We have tried to control this message rather than let it all hang out – raw, real, gutsy, and in your face.

We have sterilized Jesus and reduced the impact of His message.

We've made Him respectable, easy, and tame by giving Him a shave, cutting His hair, and placing Him in a snappy suit with polished shoes.

Jesus was rough and wild, living on people's sofas and spending His time with those the church of His day turned its back on. In reality He offended nearly everyone He met – He called religious people hypocrites and told the rich to give away their wealth. He was an incredible rebel who spoke out against injustice, organized religion, and prosperity. Jesus spoke out against religion? How can that be? He's a religious person Himself... isn't He?

Jesus didn't come to start a new religion but to give all people hope for a new future.

Hope in the middle of our struggles, mistakes, and doubts.

Hope for lives that can be little more than wearing a mask and trying to pretend everything's OK.

Hope because He loves each one of us as we are right now.

Jesus didn't come to lock people into more rules but to liberate them into a living, breathing relationship with God. Jesus was all about showing people that God could and would be present with them. John Ortberg writes in *God Is Closer Than You Think*: "The central promise in the Bible is not 'I will forgive you.' The most frequent promise is 'I will be with you'."[2] It's this that Jesus comes to reveal: not the distant God from whom we need forgiveness – although this is central to our understanding of our sin – but that God is first and foremost with us.

RELIGION

People can talk about not being into religion but still affirm their admiration of Jesus. Sometimes they may even describe themselves as "just not that religious", or say something like "I was once very religious but am not now", while at the same time admitting they quite like Jesus. It is as if being religious comprises a set of holy or devout activities, which either fits them or doesn't. What they often mean by "religion" is a pseudo-version of a faith in Jesus. It's a life based on visiting a religious building and performing some religious activities, sometimes involving singing and sometimes not.

What do we mean when we use the word "religion"? Let us look at how the implications of the word have changed over the years. Once there was a really exciting meaning before the usage that we often slip into now.

Firstly, the initial meaning: the word "religion" comes from the Old French and Latin *religio(n)* meaning obligation, bond, or reverence. But it's the Middle English word that excites me, as its original meaning was "life under monastic vows" or, as some would say, "new life under prayer". A religious life was a life that thrived under prayer, a life coming alive in prayer. I'm sure that is an understanding of the word "religion" that would excite us.

Sadly, when we speak of religion nowadays it tends to have a negative connotation. When people accuse us of "being religious" they are not talking about an exciting life of prayer; all too often they are referring to the practices and rituals that we engage in. So when I'm talking about "religion" I'm often thinking about going through the motions of faith without letting the real substance get to me. The very practices that are meant to aid us in developing our relationship with God and Jesus become the things that get in the way of that relationship.

It's a bit like getting a beautiful ornate frame to put round a valued painting and then spending so much time treating and polishing the frame that the picture inside becomes dusty, faded, and forgotten. Gradually the frame becomes the focus and the painting is lost to us.

We can do the same with our faith by simply turning up week in, week out and going through the motions. Church can be a *religious* activity or a *relationship* activity. Prayer can be a religious activity or a relationship activity. The same is true of our Bible study, worship, and community relationships.

This distorted meaning of the word "religion" is hardly positive. It is more about ritual and process than about something life-giving. It is this meaning of the word that I am now going to look at more closely.

Religion consists of all the activities and rituals we have devised to get ourselves closer to God. So if we pray more, read our Bibles more, and turn up at church more regularly, we are working out our faith. It is as though we are gaining "God chips" in some grand poker game, which we can cash in at some point.

Religion is striving to get closer to God.

Religion is "doing our bit".

Religion claims that it saves you.

Religion is the idea that God is out there somewhere and if we try hard we can draw Him closer with a "holy moment".

The central idea of "religion" is that God is somewhere else and our own activity will get us closer to Him.

Many of the religious activities we take part in have their roots in assisting us to encounter and make space for God in our lives, and have helped many people to do just that. These practices may well have grown out of a deep experience of God, and are not bad things in themselves. The problem comes, however, when we just go through the motions and rely on "religion" to bring us closer to God, without engaging in seeking God with our whole heart and letting Him disrupt our activities as we meet with Him.

> *Religious people mistakenly think that they are saving people from such things as a fruitless life, sinful sex, bad relationships, unholy humor, wayward churches, evil birth control, and what they call "strange fire." However, religion never saved anyone...*
> **Mark Driscoll**[3]

Religion is often paramount in people who are zealous for their faith; they judge people by standards of holiness that they can't even meet themselves. Saul of Tarsus was a Pharisee who studied under the leading rabbis; he wore the right clothes, he knew the Hebrew Bible off by heart and he read it in Hebrew. Saul arrested people who weren't devoted Jews. Saul was truly a religious man. But his religion wasn't saving him; he was wandering and lost, searching for a deeper sense of salvation.

Saul grew more and more zealous in the hope that he would be more and more saved. He followed "religion", trusting that by his efforts he would engage with God.

We all know people like this. It's not just in other countries that you find zealous Christians; we have them in our own churches, and they stand on street corners shouting at passers-by. Let me be clear: I'm not talking about tradition, candles, liturgy, or organs. This sense of zealousness can be found in all forms of Christianity, including my own charismatic tradition.

The charismatic tradition of church walked away from some traditional and liturgical church structures to try to find a more "authentic" Christianity, but its adherents themselves have fallen into the trap of sometimes going through the motions, like everyone else.

It's not that structure is bad, but that we can end up saying, "This is the (only/correct) way to do it." We have our prayer ministry "techniques", formed out of a desire to control the messiness of prayer and healing. Our worship has its big choruses and guitar response songs, grown from a human desire to create a religious "experience". We create rules about which is the better Bible for real exegetical preaching, and use our own religious language:

Press in to God.

Are you born again?

Bless your heart!

We don't get depressed; we have "a spirit of heaviness".

An enthusiastic Christian is "on fire for God!"

We don't have discussions; we "share".

We don't gossip; we "share prayer requests".

Is the charismatic church any less "religious" than the traditional one?

No.

Again, all these things can be excellent when they are about facilitating our relationship with God, but when they come to be about effort, or about how well we "do" it, we run the risk of making the starter the main course.

Religion is simply a way for humans to try to control God. Jesus says we need to be born in a new way. A way that revolves less around control, clocking in, saying the right words, and looking the part, and more about the simple fact that faith in Jesus is enough.

Religion is about our trying to be good and holy and earn approval. It's about our *striving* to get good or get better at being good. Jesus doesn't want us to focus on being good (though clearly He doesn't want us to be bad!), but on trusting Him to bring us from death to life.

We need to stop the doing and start the receiving. Jesus says our religion will kill us. We must stop it, drop it, and allow Him to do what is needed... to die for us. Our faith then isn't about our ability to impress but our willingness to be led by Him.

Saul met Jesus later on the road to Damascus. Many years after that he changed his name, and when he writes to the church in Philippi he's known as Paul.

Paul had done "religion"; he had got the T-shirt. He'd been through all the religious practices that were supposed to bring him closer to God but, as he states, they had got him nowhere. He had come to see that all that the religious practices had left him with was a steaming pile of garbage – even manure.

> *If someone else thinks they have reasons to put confidence in the flesh [Paul's metaphor for religious behaviour], I have more: circumcised on the eighth day, of the people of Israel, of the tribe of Benjamin, a Hebrew of Hebrews; in regard to the law, a Pharisee; as for zeal, persecuting the church; as for righteousness based on the law, faultless.*
>
> *But whatever were gains to me I now consider loss for the sake of Christ. What is more, I consider everything a loss because of the surpassing worth of knowing Christ Jesus my Lord, for whose sake I have lost all things. I consider them garbage, that I may gain Christ and be found in him, not having a righteousness of my own that comes from the law, but that which is through faith in Christ – the righteousness that comes from God on the basis of faith. I want to know Christ – yes, to know the power of his resurrection.*
>
> Philippians 3:4b–10

QUESTION: What religious practices have you found unhelpful?

QUESTION: How have you seen "religion" played out in your own life?

Time after time Jesus challenged the religious teachers of His day about their religious activity. In Luke 12 He accuses the Pharisees of being hypocrites. The word "hypocrite" comes from the Greek term *hypokrites*, which was used to describe theatre performers who wore large wooden masks. Jesus is saying that the religious leaders are like those performers, as they hide behind their masks of legalistic and ritual superiority. He is calling them out of their religion. He associates the religious life with a life of performance; it's a performance that's not real, it's pretending to be something they're not.

Back in Luke 11, Jesus goes even further with the religious people.

He's at dinner with some Pharisees when He questions their performance: He challenges them on their "religious" giving of exactly 10 per cent, which is giving without real generosity, and on their washing of items for eating but not washing their own souls, and on seeing themselves as better than others because of their "holy" behaviour. He ends with a statement that hits home to me as much as it did to them: Jesus announces that these supposedly expert religious people have in fact started to weigh others down with religious burdens that they can barely carry themselves. They have been performing for so long that they no longer recognize what is central to the faith or see that they are wearing masks.

Jesus warns them that they have forced people to live under the heavy burden of those masks and have not released them to engage in a closer relationship with God.

"Religion", for me, is the mask, the costume, the performance.

God longs for the real relationship, in which the high God becomes the close God by the grace found in Jesus.

We are in danger of confusing the two.

> **QUESTION:** What for you is the difference between "religion" and faith in Jesus?

Paul says, "My whole life, all my works, all my religion, all the rule keeping, rule making, rule enforcing, rule interpreting, once I met Jesus I realized this: It's just a steaming pile."...

Next time you're at the park... and there's a little strip of grass and a big steaming pile that somebody's dog left, just remind yourself, "Ah there lies religion..." And some religious people, they get all... "Well, my pile is more neatly stacked than your pile". So? It's still a pile. "Well, my pile's bigger than your pile". I'm not sure that's a good thing. "Well, I put sprinkles on my pile and pretended it was a cookie". Well, it's still a pile. And religion is nothing but a pile. You say, "One religion's a green pile. One religion's a brown pile. One religion's a dark brown pile." It's still a pile... And Paul says, "I realized, once I met Jesus, my whole life was just stacking a pile."

So what do you do? Where do you get righteousness? It's Jesus. This is why Jesus so passionately opposes religion. It's Jesus or religion. That's all it is. And religion says, "We must work! Something must be done!" And here's the truth. You and I, everyone who will ever be saved, is saved by works, the works of Jesus. Not our works, his works. Not what we do, what he does. Not the life we live, the life he lives.

Mark Driscoll, from "We don't need Religion; we need Jesus"[4]

SHAKING THINGS UP – DEATH TO LIFE

So what *is* "religion" and what is real faith? I would argue that religion is about bad people becoming better; faith in Jesus is about dead people coming to life.

One is based upon the Saviour but is a twisted, manipulated form of the truth.

The other is life in abundance, based not on what you do, but on the one whose help you have accepted.

It is possible for someone to attend worship, hear the stories, and even pray, yet never know the life-giving reality that is found in Jesus. It's like walking to the brink of a cliff but never seeing beyond it because of the fog.

You could say it is possible to believe in Jesus yet miss the point of Christianity.

"Religion" is ultimately the idol we use to control the uncontrollable. Jesus knew and understood this fully. This is why He challenged the Pharisees so much during His time on earth. Let's make it clear: we often speak of the Pharisees as the bad guys, but they weren't. These were people who loved God and passionately wanted to live out the Torah. But their zeal for the Torah had become codified into a set of rules for maintaining a connection to God rather than the life-changing fuel it should have been. Jesus needed to shake things up for them.

Jesus isn't about rules but about bringing us life in our death.

Where are we dying? In an addiction, a broken relationship, depression, anxiety, lies we've been caught telling, or those that haven't yet been found out? It's in these areas that God wants to be involved in bringing life, and life in all its fullness, wholeness, and richness – a life now bursting with joy and celebration in its broadest sense. Jesus calls this being "born from above".

This is what Jesus meant when He told Nicodemus that he needed to be born again. His religion was killing him; he was striving to be the best religious leader he could and it was killing him. Jesus told Nicodemus that he needed to be brought to new life. Steve McSwain of the Huffington Post website says, "**Knowing God takes no effort whatsoever.** *Effort is the baggage of religion.*"[5]

QUESTION: Do you think he's right? Is effort the baggage of religion?

QUESTION: What would the baggage be for you?

QUESTION: Do you think some effort might be needed? If so, what kind of effort?

QUESTION: Is it true that knowing God takes no effort? Don't we have to do something, or has God already done it all?

QUESTION: Is there a danger that we do nothing so we never engage with God, and thus let Him do all the work?

QUESTION: What's the danger that our efforts will become "works" of religion?

I think the truth is that Jesus has done everything we need to enable us to have this relationship with Him. We don't need "religion" or religious practices in any form to obtain a relationship with Him. The cross is a cross of grace, not a cross of obligation on our part. So on the one hand you could say that knowing God requires no effort from us; we don't need to do anything but accept it. But, on the other hand, Jesus says to those of us who realize there is a relationship to be had that we now need to join Him in picking up our own cross and following Him. We don't need "religion" but we do need to follow, which leads us to sacrifice.

Immeasurably More: Small-Group Study

QUESTION: "Religion for me is the dressing; the relationship is Jesus. We are in danger of mixing up the two." Do you agree with this? If not, why?

QUESTION: Where/when does our faith in Jesus become more like a performance than anything that's meaningful?

At this point, pray that as we read the passage the Holy Spirit would reveal to us what He is wanting to say through it.

READ: Philippians 3:1–10

What jumps out from this passage?

Do you notice something you haven't seen before or don't understand?

What is God saying to you in this reading?

QUESTION: Paul had been a hyper-religious man. Everything he had done was done in order for him to be the best religious person he could. Paul later realized when he met Jesus that everything he had been doing was rubbish in comparison to Jesus. Why is it rubbish when compared to Jesus?

QUESTION: Paul uses the word *skubalon*, which we translate as "rubbish" but is better translated as a word Christians don't often use! "Sh*t" is a strong word, which we might even describe as a vile word. But Paul uses such a strong word to make his point clear: everything is this foul compared to Jesus. Do Christians today speak this way? Are we too forgiving?

QUESTION: What rules do you live by that aren't set by Jesus but by an institution, or are unspoken rules set by a group of people?

QUESTION: What impact do these rules have on your relationship with Jesus?

QUESTION: Paul speaks of a group of people who love Jesus but still trust in works of faith to gain approval under the law of the Old Testament. In what ways are we the same today?

QUESTION: Do you know or have the faith that Paul has in Jesus? Are you able to say that everything is rubbish compared to Him?

PRAY

Pray that you will be able to leave behind anything that isn't helping your relationship with Jesus. Ask the Spirit to bring to the surface any religious thinking that you aren't aware of, and free you from it so that you can experience and understand the surpassing greatness of God.

2 BEYOND RELIGION

INTO AN AUTHENTIC RELATIONSHIP WITH JESUS

God isn't a hard rock from which we try to draw water. Sometimes God cracks the dry rock of "religion", as He did with Moses when the rock in the wilderness was split open to provide water for the people. God still does the same to meet His people and give them the water of life, but the real strength and life is found not in religious practices but in the powerful Spirit that lies behind them. Christianity is not about religion; that's what confuses people so much and makes it so complex.

Simply put... because Jesus lives, we live for Jesus.

Jesus wants us to raise our eyes above religion to the one who is truly powerful, who meets us in His Spirit.

> *Are you tired? Worn out? Burned out on religion? Come to me. Get away with me and you'll recover your life. I'll show you how to take a real rest. Walk with me and work with me – watch how I do it. Learn the unforced rhythms of grace. I won't lay anything heavy or ill-fitting on you. Keep company with me and you'll learn to live freely and lightly.*
> **Matthew 11:28–30 (MSG)**

Circle the words that jump out at you. What is the key word (or words) in this passage for you?

Jesus wants us to hand over the crumbling pieces of our religion that we cling on to, so that He can show us His "unforced rhythms of grace". How many of us just relax and breathe deeply whenever we read that phrase in this passage?

Yes, that's what I need. I need *grace*; I need this life that's to be lived freely and lightly.

Jesus has immeasurably more for us than religion and religious behaviour. He has immeasurably more... grace.

As Max Lucado put it, "God's grace has a drenching about it. A wildness about it. A white-water, riptide, turn-you-upside-downness about it. Grace comes after you."[1]

THE START OF THE STORY

When we look at the start of the big God story, we notice one thing: God created two people to live in and tend a garden. This is a beautiful garden where two beautiful people are to enjoy each other, enjoy the creation, and enjoy their intimate and personal relationship with God. The story goes that it's while God is walking around the garden looking for Adam and Eve that He notices something is wrong. Adam and Eve have sinned and are hiding from Him. This is the start of the story of God's relationship with His people. God didn't create Adam and Eve, a garden, and a church property: God created people and land. The rest was about two people living in relationship with Him. God wanted a relationship, and it was at this point that it all went wrong.

God didn't work with Abraham to start a religion but a nation, a family.

Jesus didn't come to start a religion but to bring relationship, an adoption into a family.

God isn't looking for "religious people" but for those who are willing to stand in awe, bow their knee, and dream of immeasurably more with Him. Jesus has more than religion for us; He offers vibrant, brilliant, colourful, and empowered life. Until we are willing to collapse, own up to our inability to change anything, and hold our hands up in surrender, we will only be striving on our own. But when we have hit rock bottom and realized we have nothing left, it's then that God's grace becomes all we need.

> *Something is radically wrong. Our huffing and puffing to impress God, our scrambling for brownie points, our thrashing about trying to fix ourselves while hiding our pettiness and wallowing in guilt are nauseating to God and are a flat out denial of the gospel of grace.*[2]
>
> Brennan Manning

Paul writes, "My grace is sufficient for you, for my power is made perfect in weakness. Therefore I will boast all the more gladly about my weaknesses, so that Christ's power may rest on me" (2 Corinthians 12:9).

WHOSE FAMILY ARE WE?

God's grace becomes sufficient for us when we realize we have nothing left to give. It's at this moment that, instead of striving to get into the family, we suddenly find we have already been adopted.

The biblical writers understand this relationship between Jesus and His people in a number of ways. We are sometimes called friends of Jesus, or followers, but nothing is more powerful than the image of family. Paul's writings capture this rich image of being adopted. He uses the Greek term *huiothesi*, which is generally translated as "adoption" or the "process of being adopted as sons and daughters". However, the word was more literally understood in the Greek as "adoption to sonship", and was a legal term referring to the full official standing of an adopted male heir in Roman culture. It is about taking on all aspects of inheritance and belonging. Paul uses it five times in three of his letters. Obviously, in our culture the phrase would also apply to daughtership, as even the royal family have recently changed the law governing succession to the throne!

The Spirit you received does not make you slaves, so that you live in fear again; rather, the Spirit you received brought about your adoption to sonship. And by him we cry, "Abba, Father."
Romans 8:15

Not only so, but we ourselves, who have the firstfruits of the Spirit, groan inwardly as we wait eagerly for our adoption to sonship, the redemption of our bodies.
Romans 8:23

...the people of Israel. Theirs is the adoption to sonship; theirs the divine glory, the covenants, the receiving of the law, the temple worship and the promises.
Romans 9:4

But when the set time had fully come, God sent his Son, born of a woman, born under the law, to redeem those under the law, that we might receive adoption to sonship.
Galatians 4:5

He predestined us for adoption to sonship through Jesus Christ, in accordance with his pleasure and will.
Ephesians 1:5

For Paul, this relationship with Jesus is not merely a religious transaction; it's a family adoption. We are joining a family, not a religious organization.

Joining a religious movement will do nothing but bring about striving and death.

Joining a family movement will bring about life in abundance.

- Adoption makes it clear that we are members of God's family, as a result of His saving work.

- Adoption transcends all boundaries and barriers imposed by biological and ethnic identity. Jews and Gentiles, slaves and free – all are adopted and part of the same family.

- Adoption is about individuals and whole people groups.

- Adoption implies a new identity, not the old one that has defined us.

- Adoption points to both the present reality of God's grace and the future promise of participation in God's glory.

- Adoption reminds us that God will not let us go.

THE AA RECOVERY PLAN

I have never met a more raw and honest bunch of men and women than those who attend our church Alcoholics Anonymous (AA) recovery group. Each week they come along and publicly admit their addiction, and then carefully announce their support of each other. The only commitment they ask for is that people don't keep drinking. Why are they there? They are there because they have honestly arrived at the point of exhaustion. They are acknowledging that if something doesn't change for them they have no future. They have hit rock bottom and kept on falling. I have never seen a more open and truthful bunch.

If you have never been to such a meeting, you truly are missing out, because I don't believe any regular church small group, house group or Bible-study group has ever been this real and raw. The air is thick with honesty, pain, and tears as the group pour out the truth of their mess.

This AA programme is based on the 12 steps of Alcoholics Anonymous:

- **Step One:** We admitted we were powerless over alcohol (our addiction) – that our lives had become unmanageable.

- **Step Two:** We came to believe that a Power greater than ourselves could restore us to sanity.

The steps go on in real honesty. Isn't that what church should be like? We publicly admit our addictions, problems, and sins without fear of judgment and then we come to believe in an unfathomable God who will restore us to sanity... by grace.

I think we all need some AA in our lives; some real honesty that will lead us to real grace.

In his last book, *All is Grace*, Brennan Manning describes this as "reformed and always reforming".

It is by grace that we are "recovering sinners", and the church isn't a museum of saints but a hospital for those recovering. Members of AA realize that they aren't there because they are able to save themselves but because they need someone else to save them.

> *My personal experience of the relentless tenderness of God came not from exegetes, theologians, and spiritual writers, but from sitting still in the presence of the living Word and beseeching Him to help me understand with my head and heart His written Word. Sheer scholarship alone cannot reveal to us the gospel of grace. We must never allow the authority of books, institutions, or leaders to replace the authority of "knowing" Jesus Christ personally and directly. When the religious views of others interpose between us and the primary experience of Jesus as the Christ, we become unconvicted and unpersuasive travel agents handing out brochures to places we have never visited.[3]*
> **Brennan Manning**

Jesus has immeasurably more for us than simple religion; He has a closer and deeper relationship born out of our adoption into His family. As Brennan Manning says, we need to know Jesus Christ, not just know *of* Him.

In "religion" our suffering is met by a distant God who draws close only when we pray and ask Him. In "religion" we aren't sure where we stand with this God. Is He for us or against us? Have I done enough to appease God? Do I need to do more, and then He will answer my prayers? Will He help me with my addiction if I just go to church on a Sunday?

The gospel of grace is a gospel that reminds us that it's not by our striving that we are restored, but by His. It's Jesus' work on the cross that is able to announce, "It is finished." And it is by this "It is finished" that we are able to be adopted into the family. We now have this relationship with God rather than religion.

We need to be careful that we don't accept the gospel of grace in theory but live by the gospel of religion in practice:

> *The bending of the mind by the powers of this world has twisted the gospel of grace into religious bondage and distorted the image of God into an eternal, small-minded bookkeeper. The Christian community resembles a Wall Street exchange of works wherein the elite are honoured and the ordinary ignored. Love is stifled, freedom shackled, and self-righteousness fastened. The institutional church has become a wounder of the healers rather than a healer of the wounded.*[4]
> **Brennan Manning**

God has immeasurably more available for us in this place of grace. Rather than conforming to the image of God as a "small-minded bookkeeper", God in relationship becomes an energizing power who walks with us, carries us, and sustains us. This relationship offer comes not from a transaction but from a place of profound love, and reminds us of the depth, width, and height of God's love for us. This love is truly unimaginable. Our minds can't conceive of such love because they have never experienced the like of it on earth before.

God's love makes no sense in "religion". How could it? The whole structure of "religion" is based on my striving to achieve salvation by what I do: I work hard at my religious duties and God will reward me with spiritual handouts. But love doesn't demand anything; love is given freely.

Religion, as our culture sees it, implies that God hates us and we are working to appease this hateful God. Relationship with Jesus says that we are sinful, broken, and unworthy people but God's love transcends all those barriers. God's love welcomes us into a loving relationship.

This is why religion loves law and doesn't get grace; it can't. Religion says you need it to solve your problems; real relationship says you need Jesus... grace.

BUT WHAT ABOUT PEOPLE WHO DESCRIBE THEMSELVES AS "RELIGIOUS"?

Many sincere, devoted Christians who describe themselves as "religious" are using my first definition of the word: religion – new life under prayer. Mother Teresa of Calcutta would have described herself as "religious", but what made her life so attractive was that her faith in Jesus was not built on a structure of religious striving but on a profound commitment to daily prayer. Her prayer life empowered her relationship life with Jesus.

Although Mother Teresa described herself as a Roman Catholic, this didn't define her relationship with Jesus. Her choice to be a Roman Catholic created a framework within which she could connect with God. Mother Teresa used the term "religious" but her empowering engagement with God came from her deep and sustained relationship with Him.

She once said:

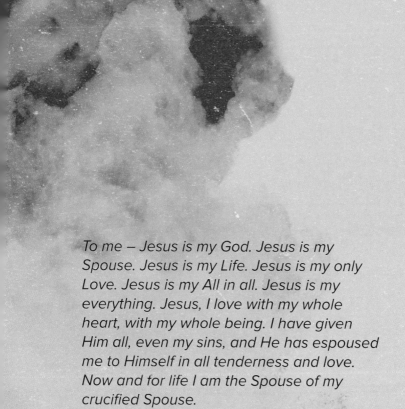

To me – Jesus is my God. Jesus is my Spouse. Jesus is my Life. Jesus is my only Love. Jesus is my All in all. Jesus is my everything. Jesus, I love with my whole heart, with my whole being. I have given Him all, even my sins, and He has espoused me to Himself in all tenderness and love. Now and for life I am the Spouse of my crucified Spouse.

Mother Teresa used the framework of her religion to bring about a transformed life and relationship with a God who is close.

Immeasurably More: Small-Group Study

QUESTION: Do you ever feel that Jesus isn't enough? When do you feel this, and what has brought you to think that?

QUESTION: What makes Jesus' death and resurrection seem so unbelievable for people? Is it that it physically couldn't happen or that it simply sounds too good to be true?

At this point, pray that as we read the passage the Holy Spirit would reveal to us what He is wanting to say through it.

READ: 2 Corinthians 12:6–10

What jumps out from this passage?

Do you notice something you haven't seen before or don't understand?

What is God saying to you in this reading?

QUESTION: Why is it that God's grace is enough?

QUESTION: What is God's "power" that is made perfect in our weakness? What would you define as His power?

QUESTION: God's grace becomes sufficient for us when we realize we have nothing left to give. Have you ever got to the point of realizing you have nothing, and all your striving and all the things around you aren't going to save you?

QUESTION: It's by God's grace that we are adopted into His family. Do you realize you can be or have been adopted? That you are a son or daughter of the King because of His grace?

QUESTION: We are recovering sinners. What sins are you recovering from?

Have you asked God to allow His grace to be sufficient for you in your sin?

QUESTION: Why does God's love not make sense in "religion" (the striving to obtain salvation through religious duties)?

PRAY

Pray that God would bring you to the point of realizing that you have nothing without Him. Offer Him all your "faith" life, asking Him to expand to fill your view so that you are able to trust Him more and know that He has everything you need. It might be that you want to offer God the areas of your life that you try to control in the mistaken hope that He will love you more if you do certain things. There is nothing you can do for God other than to fall on your knees, realize who He is, and accept that He is sufficient for you.

---

3 GOD IS CLOSER THAN YOU THINK

HEARTACHE FORCES US TO
EMBRACE GOD OUT OF DESPERATE,
URGENT NEED. GOD IS NEVER
CLOSER THAN WHEN YOUR HEART
IS ACHING.

Joni Eareckson Tada

THERE IS A FRIEND WHO STICKS
CLOSER THAN A BROTHER.

Proverbs 18:24

MONASTIC BUILDINGS

We have these strange ideas about sacred spaces. There are some places, often silent, that we perceive to be sacred or holy. Places where God dwells. Often these are remote places, with a history of meditation and prayer – we can believe that if we go to these places we will find God present.

The danger with these ideas of sacred spaces is that we must then conclude that other spaces are less sacred. People talk about "sacred" and "secular", with the latter referring to all the places where God's presence seems to be absent.

But what if your car, or your home, or your workplace, or even your children's nursery could be a place where God dwells? What if God is closer than you think?

What if God was more than a divine being dwelling in some remote place on the outer rim of the universe?

THE MOVE OF A FINGER

Before I became a church leader I spent time studying art, with the dream of becoming a filmmaker or photographer. During my study of fine art I became intrigued by a number of old masters. One painting that was particularly inspiring was *The Creation of Adam* by Michelangelo.

In 1512, Michelangelo di Lodovico Buonarroti Simoni painted a fresco based on stories from Genesis on the ceiling of the Sistine Chapel in the Vatican. This work was a masterpiece without precedent, and it went on to change the course of Western art. Its sheer scale gave it a stature unlike that of anything that had been painted before or arguably since. As you step into the chapel you don't walk up to the painting, as you do with other works; instead, it's as though you step into the frame of the picture itself.

The most famous of the panels on the ceiling is the one known as *The Creation of Adam*. It depicts God's hand reaching out to Adam's hand with only a breath's space between them. This image

of the near-touching fingers of God and Adam has become iconic of humanity and has been reproduced in countless imitations and parodies over the years. Art scholars have commented and re-commented on this scene. It's a scene that captivates people when they stand before it, not simply because of how beautifully it is painted but also because of what it shows.

In the picture, God is portrayed as reaching out to Adam with the full length of His arm. You can see in His face the effort with which He is holding out His arm to connect with Adam. You get the impression that God is, literally, at full stretch, giving it all He has – with His left arm wrapped around a heavenly being to give Him balance, because if He leant just an inch more forward He would fall. Then you look at Adam and you realize that, like many of us, he is much less committed to the presence or embrace of his Creator. He's sprawled on the ground with his arm out, but his hand is hanging slightly limp. It's as if Adam needs only to lift a finger and God would be within touching distance. It seems that God is asking us: Are *you* willing to lift your finger, because I am right here?

Could it be that God is so close that we just need to lift our finger?

PRESENT TO HIS PRESENCE

*Jesus invites us to an experience, to a taste
of the full, vibrant, dynamic, electric life of
God. Which he insists is available to every
single one of us, right here right now.*[1]
Rob Bell

Imagine you are at Great Auntie Ethel's eightieth birthday party but
would much rather be back home in bed. And then, just as you head
towards the door, you suddenly spot someone that you didn't have
a clue was there. A good friend of yours is at the party, and you
hadn't realized it because you were far too preoccupied by who you
were with, or your mind was working on your exit strategy.

I was on my hands and knees with my nine-year-old, playing with
Lego. We had each been building a spacecraft for a good while. I
have to admit that I think mine was probably the best Lego spaceship
the cosmos had seen in a good thirty years. As we sat there, Isaac
started saying to me:

"Hello, are you there?"

Of course I was; we were sitting no more than a couple of feet apart.

*"But Daddy, I've been talking to you about the Ninja Turtles for
twenty minutes and you're not listening."*

He was right; I was there but I wasn't *present*.

It was as if I was present yet absent at the same time.

There is this wonderful moment in the Exodus story when God tells
Moses to come up onto the mountain and "stay on the mountain".
It's here that God gives Moses the two stones marked with the
commandments. The English translation of the Bible doesn't always
give the full flavour of the original language, and this is an example
of such a case.

The Hebrew word *heye*, which in English we interpret as "stay with me", is in fact closer in meaning to "be". So Exodus 24:12 should read something like "Come up the mountain and be", but that doesn't make much sense in English.

God tells Moses to come up the mountain and BE with Him. Well, isn't that obvious, God? If Moses has come up the mountain then surely he's going to BE with You. The truth of it is that God knows best and He knew that He needed to tell Moses something important. God knew that once Moses arrived on the mountain top he would already be planning his route home. He'd be making lists of jobs, people to see, birthday cards to send, bills to pay, and what he was going to eat next, whereas he needed to be with God in the here and now.

We are all too eager to be moving on, heading somewhere new, and not remaining present in God's presence.

God wanted Moses to be present in His presence.

HE IS AVAILABLE

Sometimes we say that God showed up at church tonight and other times we say God wasn't in it. What we mean is *I* showed up tonight or *I* wasn't in it. We are the ones who choose to be absent or present.

Often we hope for God to "show up" in our church worship or personal prayer time. Yet the reality is that God is already present. He is available. More than that, He wants us to rest, be held, meet, recover, recharge, hear, and become aware of Him! God desires us to experience His presence, His protection, His power, His provision, and His peace, not somewhere else, but right here.

Like the father in the prodigal son story, He is there, simply waiting for us to turn up. It is we who must become aware of Him. We must become present to the presence of God.

Matthew 11:28 reads: "Come to me, all you who are weary and burdened, and I will give you rest." Wow, weary, burdened... We fit the criteria, don't we? We are tired and weighed down! But so often we overlook Jesus' invitation to enter His presence.

[heye]

CLOSER

Sometimes we are distracted from God's presence by our preoccupation with things in the world around us that seem more real but aren't. We can be preoccupied with money, women or men, friends, the football league tables, or the new episode of a baking programme. At other times we become engrossed in our own thoughts, responsibilities, worries, irritations, and preoccupations. Amidst the distractions of our lives we are absent from the one relationship that can offer us rest and sustenance. Jesus says "Come" to all who are weary and weighed down.

"Come" isn't about God moving; it's about us moving. It's about us moving in our awareness of what is already there.

God is closer than we could ever imagine.

HOW CLOSE? THE INCARNATION, LADDERS, GRIZZLY BEARS AND INNER BEINGS

So how close does this God really come? Let's look at some images of God's closeness.

1. INCARNATION

Joan Osborne said it beautifully in her song "What if God was one of us". She wrestles in this song with questions about what Jesus looked like, and what he would be like. What is particularly exciting about the incarnation isn't what Jesus physically looked like at all, but more around his character, values, passions, friendships, and his love.

The love of God is at the heart of the incarnation. The word "incarnation" is a theological word for what we call Jesus coming in flesh and blood. Jesus' life on earth is the incarnation. The incarnation isn't simply about Jesus coming to deal with sin. That would simply turn Jesus into a sin manager. The incarnation is an invitation to see God through a much more powerful lens. This lens is one that the evangelical church has ignored for far too long. Sometimes we behave as if Christmas is simply a mechanism for getting to Easter, when we will preach a proper sermon on sin. In other words, we act as if Jesus' death were the only reason for His coming to earth, and His birth and life are incidental to the story. But they're not.

The incarnation is a reminder that God does not want to love us from a distance; He wants to be with us. It's the incarnation that shows us the closeness that God wants to have with His people. God doesn't want to be the distant universe manager who sets us up and leaves us to run the programme. The incarnation is about God showing us His heart of love, His desire for relationship, and His passion for the bricks and mortar of life. He isn't a God of the spiritual but the God of the real.

*I simply argue that the cross be raised
again at the centre of the market place
as well as on the steeple of the church. I
am recovering the claim that Jesus was
not crucified in a cathedral between two
candles, but on a cross between two
thieves; on a town garbage heap; at a
crossroad so cosmopolitan that they had to
write his title in Hebrew and in Latin and in
Greek... at the kind of place where cynics
talk smut, and thieves curse and soldiers
gamble. Because that is where He died.
And that is what He died about.*[2]

George MacLeod, founder of the Iona Community

Matthew is one of the two Gospels that make a strong statement about the incarnation. The nativity scene in Matthew 1 is central to the book's theology of God's closeness. In Matthew 1:23 we are told that Mary will conceive and give birth to a son whom they will call Immanuel. The name Immanuel is a mysterious name. Many of us know it as meaning "God with us". But if we take a little time to explore and engage with the importance of this truth, Jesus as God with us, or His closeness, we are left much more aware of who this God really is.

We need to reclaim Jesus from within the walls of the church and bring Him back to where He always located Himself: in the real dirt and grit of life. It's as if Jesus has been hijacked and His image used for a totally different agenda. Jesus' agenda was real life, and we've turned it into spiritual life.

Gods have always been in the landscape of religious communities. Right from the early days of faith, when people believed that the sun, moon, and rain were all deities, these gods were always somewhere else. Sitting in a kind of green room for gods, waiting for their moment to shine. These gods were always somewhere else and our activity called them towards us. But the incarnation tells us one wild and wonderful fact about God.

He isn't like all the other gods.

He doesn't sit in the green room.

This God is fundamentally different from all the others.

He isn't over there, distant, and reclusive, but willing to be present, real, close, and near.

The second thing we learn about this God is that the incarnation is messy. We believe in a God who gets his hands dirty. Gods were always seen as not of this world. They were holy and absent except when it suited them. Not so our God, who breaks into the world into the midst of the mess of Christmas.

The Christmas story needs reclaiming. Not just from consumerism but also from being sanitized into a nice story that is just "for the children". Through the school nativity play we have successfully romanticized the incarnation. Rather than it being wild and in need of "parental guidance necessary" warnings, we have happily let Disney play with it.

Jesus was not born against the backdrop of a clean stable with neatly brushed animals and sweet, elderly shepherds, but into the tension of a violent and chaotic world.

If we were producing a more realistic version, the story would include a heurotic and psychotic warrior king murdering children to maintain his own power, and crippling political taxation imposed by the government and the religious authorities in Jerusalem.

There would have to be a religious-fundamentalist village proposing to stone a pregnant teenage girl.

We would have frightened, underpaid child labour in the form of young shepherds working in the fields at night.

There would be political refugees displaced owing to political unease between Rome and the Temple.

We would also have visitors travelling from pagan countries in the East to worship the child in accordance with their foreign religions. They certainly were not Christians.

It's in this mess that the incarnation occurs. The incarnation places God at the heart of a tormented world. It's this incarnation that tells us that God isn't scared to get dirty.

The incarnation tells us that God has a plan.

The incarnation tells us that God is *for* us and *with* us.

The incarnation tells us that this God is humble and true to who He is.

The incarnation tells us that God is closer than we think.

It's into the mess of addiction, loss, pain, self-harm, eating disorders, debt, grief, bitterness, and depression that Jesus wants to bring something new. Christmas isn't for the kids; it's for the lost, lonely, and broken, and those on their knees with no place to go.

Christmas is hope born for all people.

2. LADDERS

We have a wonderful story in Genesis 28 about a man named Jacob. Jacob isn't one of the big spiritual leaders of the Old Testament. In fact, from what we know about him he's a bit of a mummy's boy, he'd rather hang back than do any real work, and he is a thief and a liar who betrays his brother to get the family blessing. In the story, Jacob has to leave home because of his behaviour and he runs away to a "certain place". The location isn't mentioned because it doesn't really matter. It's like saying that he ran to nowhere special. This is really important for what is about to happen. Jacob is not in a sacred space, a holy place, or on any holy ground. Jacob is nowhere special.

Jacob is in the kind of place where we would spend most of our time.

Where do you spend most of your week? Workplace, home, school gates, youth club, supermarket? Wherever you pass your time is where Jacob finds himself. Nowhere special.

The sun is setting so Jacob grabs a large stone and puts it under his head to go to sleep. While he's sleeping he has a dream in which he sees a set of stairs coming down from heaven and resting on the earth. These stairs aren't waiting for him because they already have angels climbing up and down them. There at the top of the stairs is God Himself, who announces to Jacob a new promise of provision.

Jacob wakes up and declares, "Surely God was in this place and I didn't know it."

Jacob is nowhere special and he meets God, having not known He was already there.

How often do we find ourselves no place special and not realize that God is there and we didn't even know it?

This story isn't about Jacob climbing up to heaven or working to get closer to God. No, it's a story about heaven coming down to Jacob. It's a story about God being here, right here and right now in this place. Coming to a guy who is the last person you would expect God to come to: a thief, a liar, and a deceiver.

The story of Jacob tells us that God is available to us all in the most surprising places that we find ourselves.

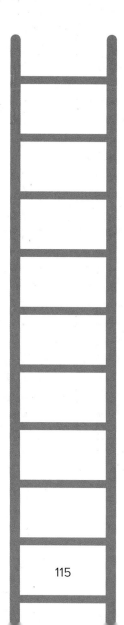

3. THE BEAR VS THE COUGAR

In 1988 a film came out called *The Bear*. I remember going to see it at the cinema and being desperate for a pet bear afterwards. In the story, a young bear cub loses his mother in a rockslide. The cub goes on to fend for himself but struggles to find food and shelter. The film cuts to elsewhere in the mountains, where a large male grizzly bear is being hunted by two men. They shoot and wound the big grizzly but he is able to get away. The two bears meet and after some time a friendship forms between them, and the grizzly takes the orphan under his wing, teaching him to fish and hunt.

As the story progresses the cub gets separated from the grizzly and is soon being watched from a distance and then confronted by a cougar intent on eating him. There is a moment in the film when you feel it's all over for the cub and his fate is going to be the same as his mother's. The cougar swipes at the cub and the cub tries to defend himself from the attack by mimicking the behaviour of his mentor, the grizzly bear. He stands on his back legs, claws extended, and struggles to sound a roar that, unlike that of the older bear, makes hardly any noise at all. Nevertheless, the cougar stops in its tracks and with fear on its face turns and slinks off in the other direction. The camera then pans round behind the cub, to what he and we couldn't see. Just behind him, standing up on its two back legs, with arms and claws out, is the big old grizzly.

The story of the bear mirrors the story of the Scriptures: whenever we are under attack, or standing alone against some ferocious threat, not far behind us is God, standing tall. The Father is always there. We might be like the little bear cub: we might not be able to see Him, might not be able to hear Him, but He is there. He's always watching; we're never alone, never unprotected. He's closer than we can imagine. Isaiah understood this when he wrote, "Whether you turn to the right or to the left, your ears will hear a voice behind you, saying, 'This is the way; walk in it.'"[3] This is a beautiful image of a God right behind us, just out of view but close enough to whisper, "This way; walk, trust me."

4. INNER BEINGS

God's presence isn't just for saints or mystics; you don't need to go to Bible school or church, because His presence is available to us at any time. God's presence isn't just around us; it's closer than that. It's as close as yourself.

The writer of the book of James says, "Draw near to God, and he will draw near to you."[4] It's that moment when we choose to step forward and find that God has already stepped forward. It's our movement that initiates a deeper realization of God's closeness.

In Ephesians 3:17 Paul writes that God wants to strengthen our inner being by His Spirit, so that Jesus may then dwell in our heart through *faith*.

God has a dwelling place that's not just in the mountain-top experiences; it's not just in "unsacred" places and it's not merely behind us. God's dwelling place is even closer than that; it's *in* us. *We* are the dwelling place of God's Spirit.

The promise is that, out of God's "glorious riches" or His overflowing abundance, He is wanting to build us up and strengthen us for this race. But what does it mean to be strengthened by God's power? So often we feel we have given out; we have served and loved, we carry the worry and burden of family life, our marriages may be struggling, and illness leaves us weakened. When God strengthens us He does it emotionally, physically, and spiritually. When God promises to strengthen us with His power He is talking about the whole of our life. We can separate out our family, social, work, and church life but God wants to strengthen it all.

The Message Bible calls this a "*glorious inner strength*".

Jesus wants to dwell in our hearts through faith. What God promises is more than a religious experience; in fact, religion was never something Jesus spoke about to His followers. Jesus wants us to have *more than religion* and invites us to jump into a living relationship with Him where the powerful Spirit is moving and dwelling in our hearts.

Time after time God announces in the Bible, "I will be with you," or, "I will never leave you." This "with you" that the writers use is closer than we could ever imagine or dream. To start separating God's closeness from our being is simply impossible. God is closer than we can comprehend.

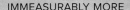

FOOTPRINTS

It has become somewhat of a Christian cliché but people genuinely love the poem about the footprints in the sand. It's a really positive image of God walking with someone on a beach, and when life gets hard God stops walking with the person and starts carrying them. People find this encouraging, this idea that God will walk with us. But God offers immeasurably more than that for us; He is able to be more to us than just someone who journeys through life with us. God doesn't want just to walk with or carry us but to be even closer than that.

People love the beach…. It gives them hope that God could be close.

PAUSE – and ask yourself for a moment…

QUESTION: What is God carrying you through at the moment?

QUESTION: How closely are you feeling Him?

QUESTION: Are you present in His presence?

QUESTION: Could God be closer than you think?

GOD'S GREAT DESIRE – DAVAQ

THE STORY OF THE BIBLE ISN'T PRIMARILY ABOUT THE DESIRE OF PEOPLE TO BE WITH GOD; IT'S THE DESIRE OF GOD TO BE WITH PEOPLE.[5]

God's desire is to be with us. Religious pursuit comes from the desire for us to "get" closer to Him; God's desire is simply to be close to us.

When we think about the closeness of God we sometimes struggle to comprehend the nature of this presence. We speak of Him walking alongside us and of His company being like that of an old friend. But the closeness that the Bible speaks of is much more profound than that. The writer of Psalm 139 says there is no place we can go to be away from His presence. He writes that God is closing in on him, behind and in front of him. He also says God's hand is upon him.

God's presence is as close as an intimate touch.

The writer of Proverbs makes the argument that God is even closer than a touch. Proverbs 18:24 reads, "One who has unreliable friends soon comes to ruin, but there is a friend who sticks closer than a brother." There is a friend who is closer than flesh and blood. The Hebrew word used here for close is *davaq*, which is used only three times in the Bible.

Davaq is one of those words that translate beautifully into many fragments and senses. It can be translated as "cling", as in cling on to something; other versions say "abiding" or "remaining", and still others have translated it as "loyalty stemming from a place of affection". But this word means more than close emotional support. It is better understood as a physical proximity sustained by a bond. So we translate it in the Bible as "being joined together" or "sticking closer", but the intended image is that of two things pressed up against each other, or intertwined.

In other words, God's closeness isn't a case of His presence propping us up, or leaning up against us, but one of Him and us being intertwined, connected, and knotted together.

God is thus much closer even than a presence around us; He and we are interwoven. The line between Him and us is so blurred that it's hard to prise the two apart. This has many implications when we start thinking about our adoption, being a holy people, and how we live in the world. It's Christ tangled up with me that makes me holy. As Paul puts it in Galatians 2:20, "I have been crucified with Christ and I no longer live, but Christ lives in me."

We are often in danger of doing what the Gnostics and the Greeks did many years ago when they created the idea of secular places and sacred spaces. We also divide secular life from sacred life. We set these two aspects up as opposites in contrast. But if God is *davaq*, so close that He is intertwined with us, then there can't be two separate aspects of our life, because the sacred God is making our life and our very being sacred.

In being so close to us He joins us in our struggles, sufferings, and pain and we join Him in His beauty, wholeness, and holiness. God is closer than we think and at the same time we are closer to God than we think.

BENEDICTION

In chapter 6 of the book of Numbers there is a wonderful benediction or blessing that the priests are given to say over God's people. It's a blessing of God's presence and closeness.

God said to Moses that he should bless God's people like this...

> *"The Lord bless you, and keep you.*
> *The Lord make his face shine upon you*
> *and be gracious to you;*
> *the Lord turn his face towards you and give*
> *you peace."*
> Numbers 6:24–26 (MSG)

This blessing was used early in the morning and late at night. The priest would stand with hands raised, representing God, and speak these words over the people. The words are intriguing and rather mysterious. God's face turning and shining could sound rather eerie and cryptic. But it is simply a way of God saying that's He's with you. If someone's face is turned towards you then you have their attention; they are aware of you and they are attentive to you and your needs. God's face is attentive to you right now.

Many of us will have heard this many times but may still feel that there is a gap between our knowledge about God and His closeness and our actual awareness and experience of His presence.

When I was teaching Isaac to ride his bike when he was seven, I would take him out along the canals around London. The towpaths aren't that wide so we would end up cycling one behind the other. When we first went out, Isaac would be riding his bike no more than a couple of metres in front of me but because I was behind him he couldn't see me. He would end up shouting, "Are you watching me?" and "Are you facing me?" His concern was that I would be looking round at the boats, birds, and wildlife rather than focusing on him. He would get stressed, stop, and turn round to see where I was. Often this would almost end in a head-on collision, forcing me to brake suddenly.

Eventually Isaac would be off on his way, reassured that I was there, but it wouldn't be long before he would once again shout, "Dad, are you watching me; are you facing me?" I would call back, "I'm here, Isaac. I'm watching; it's OK. Keep going; I've got my eye on you." Knowing I was near him, watching, he would cycle on again, content. My face was turned towards Isaac and he knew safety and peace. God's face is turned towards us, too, and because of this we can experience His peace.

HOW DO WE PUT IT INTO PRACTICE?

So how do we engage practically with the God of immeasurably closer presence? Well, the answer is simple: we need to go deeper...

FINGER PRAYER

This prayer was inspired by the insulation tape "Sistine Chapel" hands, which can be found in the Bless Network prayer room in France:

> *When I can't let go #scared*
> *I choose to lift my finger to touch your*
> *outstretched hand*
> *the God who never lets go*
>
> *When I can't be arsed #lazy*
> *I choose to lift my finger to touch your*
> *outstretched hand*
> *the God who speaks life*
>
> *When I can't keep my eyes open #tired*
> *I choose to lift my finger to touch your*
> *outstretched hand*
> *the God who never sleeps*
>
> *When I can't see a way forward #stuck*
> *I choose to lift my finger to touch your*
> *outstretched hand*
> *the God who makes the path straight*
>
> *When I can't find time #busy*
> *I choose to lift my finger to touch your*
> *outstretched hand*
> *the God who walks at 3mph*

When I can't stop #addicted
I choose to lift my finger to touch your
outstretched hand
the God who breaks through

When I can't get something out of my head
#burden
I choose to lift my finger to touch your
outstretched hand
the God whose unforced rhythm is grace

When I can't find the strength #drained
I choose to lift my finger to touch your
outstretched hand
the God who fights for us

When I can't find peace #stressed
I choose to lift my finger to touch your
outstretched hand
the God who displaces worry at the center
of my life

Amen.

This prayer was written by Matt Long of Bless[6]

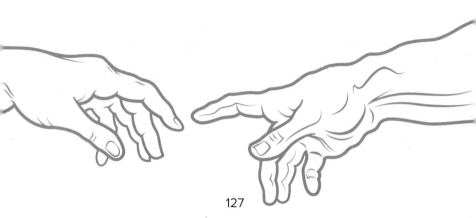

Immeasurably More: Small-Group Study

QUESTION: When do you feel that God's presence is missing? Has there been a moment when you have thought "Where is God?"?

QUESTION: Is feeling God close as important as knowing that He is close? What's the difference, and which do you think is the more important to you?

QUESTION: Are you able to speak of a time when God felt distant, and you couldn't feel Him, but you knew deep down He was present with you?

At this point, pray that as we read the passage the Holy Spirit would reveal to us what He is wanting to say through it.

READ: Ephesians 3:14–19

What jumps out from this passage?

Do you notice something you haven't seen before or don't understand?

What is God saying to you in this reading?

QUESTION: What do you think it means to have God dwelling in your heart? Are you able to explain it further?

QUESTION: Paul says that God wants to strengthen us by His Spirit in our innermost being. How do you think this happens? Is it a simple encouragement by the Spirit or is it a physical strengthening? Could it be both?

QUESTION: Paul speaks again about faith and not religion or religious practices. Paul understood that as we step out and trust in Jesus, His death, and His resurrection, then through this faith God is expanded in us as we make ourselves less important. How have you experienced this in your own life?

QUESTION: Has there been a time when you have felt God as close as in your innermost being?

QUESTION: Do you think it's possible to experience God as closer than ourselves? Why or why not?

QUESTION: Could God be closer than we think and we didn't even know it?

PRAY

Pray that God would help you to become more aware of Him and help you to become "present to His presence". Give God permission to be closer than you have ever imagined, allowing Him more rule in your life, heart, and body. Maybe tell God why you sometimes hold Him at arm's length – what are you protecting? You might also want to tell Him of your frustration at not sensing Him at the most difficult times.

A Deeper Story
A real story about a person called Christian

Life was always great. Perfect parents, a great church, and amazing friends. I had nothing to complain about as I went through my teenage years, and I set off for university ready for all it could throw at me. On arriving in Durham, I didn't realize how shallow my faith was. It had always been there but had been maintained for me by others. I had been taken to Christian events and shown what to believe by my youth leaders and friends, so had never needed to do the hard work of digging down and making it mine.

I didn't realize it until a year after university but my faith was rootless. I'd not really invested in finding a church while I was there and had spent most Saturday nights out partying with friends. I was like spiritual tumbleweed, blown all over the place, and suddenly found myself working harder and harder to try to keep going. Work was hard and my boss was pressing me to achieve results.

It was about this time that I hit a huge wall of depression. Life became dark and hopeless, and I struggled to get out of bed each day. Days became shorter as I stayed in bed longer. As time went by I realized that my depression wasn't due to my lack of spiritual depth, but I had to realize that my lack of roots had dried me out. My faith was more about religious affiliation than about drinking deep of God's presence. The stresses of life and the anxiety I was living with became exacerbated by my shallow faith. I was very much a Christian but a Christian who was empty and had no roots to hold me firm in the storms of life.

It was at this point that I did a few things. I went to see a Christian counsellor, who helped me explore my anxiety. I started to pray with other Christians, who asked for me to be filled afresh with the Holy Spirit. At first it was as if I was so hard that the Spirit bounced right off me, but their prayers and invitations to the Holy Spirit soon softened me for a new awakening to God. The final thing I did was to begin to invest in my faith myself. I started to pray and wait on God regularly, trying to do this daily but not feeling guilty when I didn't manage it. I would read my Bible and hear God speak to me through it; I would also invest in a daily rhythm of deepening my worship life. **The more I adored God in worship, the closer He came, and the deeper my faith grew.**

Depression still hovers somewhere on the edge of my vision, but my roots in God have taken me to a place of trusting and relying on Him. I've realized that without roots that draw what I need from God all I am ever going to do is draw upon myself, and this isn't going to sustain me. This adventure is a daily one of making the effort to drill down into the life of the Spirit to sustain, grow, and mature my faith in Jesus.

MOVEMENT
THREE
DEEPER

AND I PRAY THAT YOU, BEING
ROOTED AND ESTABLISHED
IN LOVE, MAY HAVE POWER,
TOGETHER WITH ALL THE LORD'S
HOLY PEOPLE, TO GRASP HOW
WIDE AND LONG AND HIGH AND
DEEP IS THE LOVE OF CHRIST,
AND TO KNOW THIS LOVE THAT
SURPASSES KNOWLEDGE – THAT
YOU MAY BE FILLED TO THE
MEASURE OF ALL THE FULLNESS
OF GOD.
Ephesians 3:17–19

Roots have to grow down before a tree can grow up. Having thought about God's majesty and power and then His closeness, we come to Movement Three, "Deeper". In this movement we will be thinking through three areas of spiritual discipline to help us be rooted and established in all that God has for us. First, we will consider how we grow in God by sinking our roots into Him and drinking His living water through prayer. We will then look at the spiritual discipline of waiting on God's presence before reminding ourselves finally that the Holy Spirit isn't just for the early church but also for today, and therefore there needs to be a daily commitment of saying yes to God.

1 ROOTS

In our house, plants just don't last. People come to visit and realize there isn't any living thing growing in our home, and presume it's because we have never been given anything. So they return with a nice green thing, telling us it's dead easy to look after. Dead easy? Really? They have obviously never lived with us. A few years ago I had a cactus. It died from lack of water. "But cacti don't need much water!" I hear you cry. We still killed it. The truth is, we forget to water any plant we have and eventually we notice it's going brown and we try to give it some liquid, but it's often too late. It's the strength of the roots and the number of them that help a plant to live as long as it can. Plants with small shallow roots die if not given much attention, but plants with longer and deeper roots can last much longer, as they can gather as much as possible of the moisture available to them. We are no different.

We try to behave like cacti, but we are actually water-hungry houseplants. We need regular watering to avoid becoming dehydrated. We need to be constantly filled and refilled in order to thrive.

C. S. Lewis writes that:

> *If you want to get warm you must stand near the fire: if you want to be wet you must get into the water. If you want joy, power, peace, eternal life, you must get close to, or even into, the thing that has them. They are not a sort of prize which God could, if He chose, just hand out to anyone. They are a great fountain of energy and beauty spurting up at the very centre of reality. If you are close to it, the spray will wet you: if you are not, you will remain dry.*[1]

If we want to be warm we need to stand near the fire; if we want water we need to get ourselves close to the water's source.

Paul writes to the church in Ephesus that they need to be "rooted" and established in love.[2] It's this rooting that sets them up, that establishes them in something wonderful. He tells the Ephesians that if they don't root themselves in love, eventually they will be blown over or knocked down and will die. It's the roots of a plant that create a solid foundation for the plant to thrive.

Much of the history of the people of God had involved their being rootless in one way or another. There was the nomadic beginning, roaming around looking for a land of their own before being enslaved in Egypt and then spending many more years wandering around the desert. They then found the promised land and some roots, but before long were once again taken into exile, this time to Babylon. Eventually God's people returned to Jerusalem to try to reclaim some sense of who they were. That was before they found themselves being occupied by the Romans in the first century BC. Christianity then followed, and as it grew it made its way to Ephesus. Central to its belief was that it was Jesus and not the land that we needed to root ourselves in, because the world was an unstable, changing place.

The Ephesians knew this, as did people in many other areas of the Middle East. Life, business, and politics were moving fast, and everything was becoming a greater struggle. Paul writes to the church that they need to be rooted and firmly established in love.

What does love look like? Jesus.

The word "rooted" comes from the Greek term *rhizoo*, meaning "to become strengthened", with an emphasis on the *source* of such strength, not the *act* of putting down roots. It's like saying, "Make sure you are planted firmly in rich soil." The word *rhizoo* also appears in Colossians 2:7, but this time it is translated as "being strengthened and built up in him".

[rhizoo]

to become strengthened

The writers of the Bible use images that reference earlier accounts of the story of God's people. Sometimes it is a shorthand way of implying more than is said. It's as if the writer is saying something that is true for now, but if we look back we see that it was also true then. By noticing this, the readers can ask the question, "What is Paul not saying but alluding to?" In this passage from Ephesians Paul's use of the word "root" is considered by many theologians to be a "nudge nudge, wink wink" to an earlier prophetic image found in Jeremiah.

> *This is what the LORD SAYS:*
>
> *"Cursed is the one who trusts in man,*
> *who draws strength from mere flesh*
> *and whose heart turns away from the LORD.*
> *That person will be like a bush in the wastelands;*
> *they will not see prosperity when it comes.*
> *They will dwell in the parched places of the desert,*
> *in a salt land where no one lives.*
>
> *"But blessed is the one who trusts in the LORD,*
> *whose confidence is in him.*
> *They will be like a tree planted by the water*
> *that sends out its roots by the stream.*
> *It does not fear when heat comes;*
> *its leaves are always green.*
> *It has no worries in a year of drought*
> *and never fails to bear fruit."*
> Jeremiah 17:5–8

Paul is reminding his readers of the prophet Jeremiah's image of the two plants with two different sources of strength: one that provides fruit, and the other that doesn't.

1. BUSHES IN WASTELANDS

Jeremiah says that some people are like bushes in a wasteland. First of all, what is this wasteland? Jeremiah gives us the answer in the lines above. He writes that these cursed little bushes are like people who have planted themselves in the belief that humankind has the answers. They trust in what people can offer and so they are drawing what they think they need from the strength found in mere flesh.

"Flesh" in the Bible is a metaphor for all that we offer ourselves: our own ideas, our own hopes and dreams. It means depending on our own knowledge and wisdom to make good decisions. It is also the physical aspect of who we are, which distinguishes us from God: it's a symbol of our sinful human nature in contrast to God's perfection. Flesh is a symbol of our mortality, our weakness, our imperfection, our powerlessness, our worldly standards, and our bent towards sinning.

Jeremiah is saying that some of us plant ourselves in our own mess and hope that it's going to give us the sustenance we need. But this land is nothing but waste; it's nothing but dry desert; it's nothing but salty, useless earth.

2. TREES BY STREAMS

Jeremiah then contrasts the bush with a tree. Trees behave totally differently from bushes. Bushes have shallow roots but trees have big, strong roots that grow towards the water. Each year the tree grows bigger and stronger, developing its roots to form a network of access points for the water needed for continued life and growth.

Jeremiah writes that those who are blessed are the ones who trust in God and have confidence not in themselves but in Him. Jeremiah says that those who are plugging themselves into the source of all things will find that they are planted next to a water supply that will give them what they really need.

He says that if we establish ourselves with deep roots in God then, like a tree, we will find that when drought comes we will have nothing to fear, because our roots go deeper than those of a bush and thus we will have access to water even when there is none on the surface. Which means our leaves will be greener, we don't have to worry about desert seasons, and we will never fail to bear fruit.

For Jeremiah, the stream that is providing water in this context is God Himself. It's from our faith that we then receive the life-giving Spirit. Jesus used the water of life image later in His teaching.

In John 4 Jesus meets a Samaritan woman whose life is a mess by Jewish standards. She has been married five times and when Jesus encounters her she is living with her boyfriend – this means that she is socially and spiritually excluded from her culture, leaving her as a "dry bush" separated from the water source.

"Jesus answered her, 'If you knew the gift of God and who it is that asks you for a drink, you would have asked him and he would have given you living water... but whoever drinks the water I give them will never thirst. Indeed, the water I give them will become in them a spring of water welling up to eternal life' " (John 4:10, 14).

The Samaritan woman soon realized who Jesus was and then received this living water. Her response was to run off and tell everyone she knew.

Let's take a moment and notice something in the Jeremiah reading. In this picture painted for us by Jeremiah, where is the tree planted? We know it's planted next to a stream, but we need to look at what the wider landscape is like.

It does not fear when heat comes;
its leaves are always green.
It has no worries in a year of drought
and never fails to bear fruit.

Unexpectedly, the tree and the bush are both planted in a harsh environment. They both feel the heat, they are both burning in the sun, and the desert land is suffering from drought. But the tree has more than the bush; it has deep, strong roots that tunnel to the source of water, the source of life.

TREE QUESTIONS

It is interesting to consider the difference between trees growing in hot, dry climates and those that grow in damp, wet climates. Which ones have the deeper roots?

Trees growing where it rains a lot and where the land is wet will often have shallow roots, as they don't need to venture down to find the water buried deep in the earth – unlike the trees growing in the dry places, which have to grow deep roots.

So which trees are stronger in high winds?

A tree that experiences long dry seasons will send its roots down deep to reach a constant source of water that doesn't depend on the weather. This image of the tree sending its roots deep and wide in order to remain strong in hard times is such a powerful image for us as Christians.

FRUIT

Jeremiah ends his metaphor by saying that someone who plants roots that tap into the source will be a tree that grows much fruit. Bushes with few, shallow roots don't bear much fruit, maybe a few berries, but trees with deep roots will bear a lot of fruit. We are going to look at fruit later, but for now let's just say that it's the trees that have healthy roots that grow and multiply fruit. It's the healthy trees that produce more. And trees that are plugged into the living water source will produce healthy fruit, immeasurably more fruit than can be imagined.

GROWING ROOTS
FOR YOU WILL NURSE AND BE SATISFIED AT HER COMFORTING BREASTS; YOU WILL DRINK DEEPLY AND DELIGHT IN HER OVERFLOWING ABUNDANCE.
Isaiah 66:11–13

If we were to ask for a show of hands on how many of us feel that we need more of something, and that our roots need some help to really tap into the source, many if not all of us would vote with a resounding yes. Few of us feel that we are making it into the good stuff. We've tasted and seen but we've not drunk deeply of it. We've sipped but not become legless on the Spirit. I want what the disciples experienced at Pentecost. I want people to wonder whether I've been drinking at the pub at 8 a.m. I want to be *that* well watered by the living water.

It was in David's heart to pursue deeper roots and deep rehydration. In Psalm 42:7 he writes:

Deep calls to deep
in the roar of your waterfalls;
all your waves and breakers
have swept over me.

The image we have here is of God as a powerful source of the Spirit. Deep waters call to even deeper ones. This water thunders with power and it's washing over the psalmist like the powerful waves out at sea. The idea is one of David being caught up in a powerful rush of living water. Nourishing water. This isn't someone sipping politely on the Spirit but being battered and overrun by it.

David in the Psalms writes again and again about thirsting and seeking this kind of refreshing. Psalm 63:1–3 reads:

God, you are my God,
earnestly I seek you;
I thirst for you,
my whole being longs for you,
in a dry and parched land
where there is no water.
I have seen you in the sanctuary
and beheld your power and your glory.
Because your love is better than life,
my lips will glorify you.

David realized that roots need to grow, and for roots to grow there needs to be a time of *earnestly seeking* God. Roots don't just appear; you don't wake up in the morning and find that you've gained some. Roots need the hard work of drilling down and earnestly pursuing the living water.

Why is it that when someone becomes a Christian they can be so full of life, but then months later they start to feel the strain of their newfound faith? The truth is that when we become a Christian it's like experiencing a drink from this water, and it's so, so, good that it carries us for a time. But we leak, we give out, and we give away. We become dehydrated and we need to start the hard work of building in a daily rhythm of tapping into the source. We've tasted the source and now God wants us to have more than a taste.

The danger is that this can start to sound like striving and struggling on our part and even like doing religious activities. But this isn't about ritual or hard work; it is about creating roots for ourselves that allow us to thrive and not just survive. God wants more for us than existing; He wants thriving. Thriving is about flourishing, blooming, and growing. It is about us producing good fruit. It's about our health.

Plants that grow roots then drink and thrive.

Plants that don't grow roots can't drink and therefore don't thrive!

A SEEKING PRAYER

MY BOOTS SQUELCH ON WATERLOGGED GRASS
WATER FROM BENEATH THE SURFACE WELLS UP
AND BREAKS FORTH
SPILL OUT, SPIRIT OF GOD
SATURATE ME

MY EYES SEE THE FIRST SHOOTS OF SPRING
SEED FROM BENEATH THE SURFACE WAKES UP
AND BREAKS THROUGH
STIR, SPIRIT OF GOD
SPRING UP IN ME

MY HEART SENSES THE STILL SMALL VOICE
SPIRIT WHO HOVERS OVER THE SURFACE WHISPER
AND BREAK IN
SPEAK, SPIRIT OF GOD
SILENCE ME

AMEN

MATT LONG, THE BLESS COMMUNITY[3]

HOW DO WE GROW THESE ROOTS?

Luke 8:13 says, "The seeds that fell on rocky ground are the people who gladly hear the message and accept it. But they don't have deep roots, and they believe only for a little while. As soon as life gets hard, they give up" (CEV).

We can hear what God has to say to us and we can get really excited about it, but we don't always allow it to change us or develop us. We are masters of the superficial and the surface level. Look at our homes. Most modern furniture is rootless furniture. Such furniture looks like solid wood, but it's not. It has a wood veneer, but under the surface it's all little chips of broken wood. It is wood, but at the same time it's not.

As we saw earlier, Jesus said that the Pharisees were religious performers; their faith consisted of going through the motions of a relationship with God, but they wore masks. We need to make sure that we don't act in the same way, looking spiritual on the surface but not letting it go any deeper.

Do we really want to be that way? No! We want to be a deep people with secure roots, not shallow people with bush-sized roots. We want to be people who drink deeply of the living water through those deep roots, so that when the wind comes we can hold on and thrive.

When the rough winds come and perhaps somebody in your family gets ill or dies, the trial won't blow you away, because you've got roots.

So how do you go about this deep drinking from the source?

First, you've got to spend time **alone with God**, and, second, you've got to spend time **with other believers**. Without a daily drink from the source, we dry up and get swept away when the pressure is on. Without the roots we can't handle the wind, which comes to test us. It's the act of sitting and resting in God's presence, being present to His presence, noticing His closeness, that gives us the time to drink from Him. Some people do this with daily Bible reading and prayer. Some play music; others keep a journal. Whatever your preferred way of doing it, it needs to be done.

"Whatever it takes to keep the focus on God, do it!"[4]

DAILY, WEEKLY, ANNUALLY

Rick Warren talks about "diverting daily, withdrawing weekly and abandoning annually".

- **Diverting daily** is about regularly finding short spaces of time to rest with God, which might include reading the Bible or other spiritual books, and praying.

- **Withdrawing weekly** is about making sure that each week you have a significant time to meet with God. This could be church on a Sunday if you are not giving out at it. If you are, then another time will be needed for you to withdraw into His presence.

- **Abandoning annually** is about getting away on retreat or a spiritual holiday to invest deeply in your relationship with God. This is about hiding away somewhere that will restore your soul and help you regain the wonder. This is about having a significant space of time to dig deep into all that God has for you, so you come away ready for the year ahead.

It's through regularly creating space to invest in this relationship that roots can grow. Some people will respond to this by saying, "That sounds a lot like 'religion' to me; didn't we talk about that in Movement Two?" But this rhythm isn't about ritual or religion; it's about connection and investment in order to deepen this relationship with the God of more.

And it's through personally investing in and learning from a community of people of faith that we encounter the living water together and enable our roots to go deeper.

Being Honest

QUESTION: We are gifted at making excuses for not spending time with God. How does your diary or time management need to change so that you can spend more time with Him?

QUESTION: What have you promised yourself in the past that you would do to invest in growing roots that you have never completed or maybe even started?

QUESTION: Why do you think God wants us to invest in growing our roots into Him? Why are the struggle and hard work important?

Immeasurably More: Small-Group Study

QUESTION: How shaky does your faith sometimes feel? What is it that anchors you to the ground and keeps you plugged into God?

QUESTION: If you were a plant, do you feel as if you'd have shallow roots or deep, strong roots? Why is this? It could be because of a tragedy in your life, because you've only been a Christian for a short time, or because you've never really been allowed to develop your own personal faith.

At this point, pray that as we read the passage the Holy Spirit would reveal to us what He is wanting to say through it.

READ: Jeremiah 17:5–8

What jumps out from this passage?

Do you notice something you haven't seen before or don't understand?

What is God saying to you in this reading?

QUESTION: As Jeremiah writes, some people find strength in mere flesh. What does he mean by "the flesh"?

QUESTION: Jeremiah says that some people's faith has shallow roots in what is an already dry land. Do you identify with this image or not?

QUESTION: Why does Jeremiah say someone is cursed if they trust in the wrong things? Is there a better way in which you could explain what Jeremiah means by "cursed"?

QUESTION: How does a person develop deeper, stronger roots?

QUESTION: What do you think is the stream that Jeremiah is speaking of? Have you experienced this stream before?

QUESTION: How do you regularly create space to make sure you are investing in your relationship with God? Are you seeing your roots deepen?

QUESTION: What is getting in the way of your roots growing? Do you need to make some changes to see them have the space to grow?

PRAY

Rather than praying a "shopping list "of items to give to God, why not simply wait on Him? Give God some time to speak back to you. Sit in silence and wait, keeping your attention on what He might be saying or doing in or with you. Try not to clog up the time with words, but sit in silence and allow Him to show you His presence and give you a deep, refreshing drink from His stream.

2 SITTING – WAITING

It's all too easy to get what we think we need from the shallow spirituality of magazines and New Age movements. We can dip our toes into what God has for us, which often gives us just enough to get through the day.

The world can try to sell us an alternative to God's presence. It's as if we have created cheap replicas or fake alternatives to something so powerful, colourful, and true. We might buy our mothers pampering spa days as a refreshing break, but this kind of experience gives only a shallow and short renewal.

The reality is that this way of sustaining ourselves isn't realistic; it's short-lived and requires us to hunt and search in pools that aren't even clean.

Developing practices that can sustain us, that allow us to drink deep and encourage our roots to flourish, is the key to our progress. The reason the church feels dehydrated is that we are masters of doing and not so good at stopping for refreshment. Often we are so busy that we don't realize that we're being active with no real power. It's as if we are limping along unaware that there is a problem.

The truth is that roots take time to grow. Children can be frustrated because they want to be sixteen but are still only six, but as adults we know that those years of growing and struggling are the making of us. It's in the struggle that we have become who we are now.

Jesus was fully aware of our need to sit and rest in His presence for our roots to feed on the God of immeasurably more.

WORKING AND RESTING

In Luke 10 we have the mesmerizing story of Mary and Martha. Jesus and His disciples are packed into a small living room in Bethany. The home belongs to His friends Mary, Martha, and Lazarus, the one whom He raised from the dead.

The room is full of people squashed onto every possible surface, and Mary is sitting at Jesus' feet, listening intently to all that He has to say. Mary is gripped; she's listening and learning, not wanting to miss a moment of her friend Jesus speaking. She wants to drink deep from this well. On the other hand, Martha is so preoccupied by making sure people are comfy and well fed that she is present in the same house as Jesus but not present *to* Him. Martha is distracted by all that she has to do. Having had enough of working on her own she stomps into the room, and, in what I imagine is a stroppy voice, cuts into the teaching. She may have been standing at the edge for a while waiting for a pause, but it's not come, so in her frustration she just jumps in: "Lord, don't You care that my sister has left me to do the work by myself? Tell her to help me!" Jesus responds calmly and clearly: "Martha, Martha, you are worried and upset about many things, but few things are needed – or indeed only one. Mary has chosen what is better, and it will not be taken away from her."

Most of us are good at being a Martha, but not as good at being a Mary.

Despite all the beneficial things Martha was doing for Jesus and His disciples, Jesus said that Mary had chosen the best place to be at that moment. To just sit at His feet and do nothing: to be with Him and listen. We call this "active rest".

Listening is the active part.

Doing nothing is the resting part.

WAITING

We're a generation of rushers; we want everything immediately, and then wonder why life feels so shallow. There is a reason why we feel empty and shallow: we're lacking the one thing that we truly need. This one thing we need is the one thing we can't rush, pressurize, or make happen. The one thing that truly encourages us, empowers us, and gives us our fulfilment comes from the one person we can't manipulate or trick.

I have this friend who is an über-awesome retired priest. He's the kind of man who oozes God's presence. All the young guys we are training for ministry are sent to spend a few hours with him to sit at his feet (not literally!) and hear about his lifelong ministry. Until his retirement he worked in the East End of London for over twenty-five years. I was talking with him on one occasion about wanting to make sure that in thirty years' time I am still running the race well and am just as excited about all that God is doing as I am today. My fear is that I will burn out and become discouraged and cynical because of my inability to truly trust God. If I wasn't a Christian I would be a workaholic; I would be discouraged in a second and become a habitual cynic. I know this to be true because it's a battle I fight each day. I asked Fr Duncan how he has carried on all these years, serving and loving people without becoming tired, jaded, and half-hearted. His response wasn't quite what I expected.

He replied, "Each morning I get up, I sit in my chair and I wait on God. I wait for His Spirit to come and fill me and then from that place I get up and move through the day."

With a confused look on my face I asked what happened if he had a meeting. He responded that he did nothing until he had been filled with the Spirit, and if God didn't show up, he would just keep waiting.

He had recently missed a meeting with me, and this is why. He'd been waiting on God and needed to keep waiting.

Psalm 27:14 puts it beautifully: "Wait for the Lord; be strong and take heart and wait for the Lord."

I'm not sure that I want to wait. I'm a bit too busy to wait. You would think that God would be on time for a meeting. He's God; surely He has an alarm clock? Why would He keep us waiting?

That's the point, though, isn't it? He's God and we're not. We want the instant, the immediate, and the quick. But God teaches us that we are human "beings" and not human "doings".

So I am learning again to wait.

But they who wait for the Lord
shall renew their strength;
they shall mount up with wings like eagles,
they shall run and not be weary,
they shall walk and not faint.
Isaiah 40:31 (ESV)

The reality is that we are in good company if we wait on God. The Scriptures are full of people doing just this.

Joseph waited **fifteen years**.

Abraham and Sarah waited **twenty-five years**.

Moses waited **forty years**.

Hannah waited many, **many years**.

Elizabeth waited at least **sixty years**.

Jesus waited **thirty years**.

The Bible is the resounding story of "If God is making you wait, you're in very good company". Waiting is central to many of the biblical stories. The disciples had to wait for forty days to experience the Holy Spirit, but we struggle to wait four minutes. If God takes longer than that we think He's obviously not coming. Waiting is a symbol of our desperation for immeasurably more. The Lord is saying to His people today:

"When you come looking for me, you'll find me. Yes, when you get serious about finding me and want it more than anything else, I'll make sure you won't be disappointed… I'll turn things around for you."
Jeremiah 29:13–14 (MSG)

Waiting on God is His way of finding out how serious we are. When we say we've been waiting on God, what we often mean is that we've "waited" a little for God. How desperate are we really for the immeasurably more? We want the more without the work of waiting. We want it to be like turning on a tap rather than the hard work of rooting ourselves into a stream.

The longer we wait on God, the more we realize that the fabric of life involves waiting. The whole of life is a process of waiting. We wait to leave school, we wait to get a job, we wait to get married, we wait to have children, we wait for healing, and so on. It's during these times of waiting that God is breaking our spirit of self-dependence and awakening our spirits to the reality of our persistent need. Waiting is about our realizing that nothing is in our hands but everything is in His.

But waiting on God isn't about doing nothing; waiting on God is about the active work of becoming present to Him. When the disciples met in the upper room and the Holy Spirit came, they had been there for forty days. In that time they had waited and prayed. It hadn't been forty days of twiddling their thumbs. Yes, they had made the dubious decision to vote in a replacement for Judas rather than waiting to see what Jesus wanted them to do about replacing him. But this time was about waiting. It was this waiting that meant they were attentive to the Spirit's coming. It was through waiting that they – and we – are aware of God's presence.

Waiting builds intimacy with and dependence upon God. As we wait we become reliant on Him; less of us, more of Him.

The reason we are able to read about the great men and women of the Bible is that they all had one thing in common. They were all people who learned that their success in life was directly proportional to their intimacy with and dependence on God. For them, a relationship with God wasn't a get-rich-quick scheme. For many of them, it was a matter of life and death.

GOD NEVER ASKS US TO WAIT WITHOUT HIM

As we look at difficult times in the Bible – Abraham with Hagar, Moses killing the Egyptian, David and Bathsheba – we realize that it was during these testing times that God's people developed their relationship with Him. Some of the most intimate and profound relationships were born out of times of "doing life" with God in the trenches. The helpful truth is that we are able to read of people waiting and searching after God. These stories are all about people who by the end have grown and developed in the process with God and the promise of God. God is as interested in the waiting as He is in the final goal of being rehydrated by His Spirit.

We might focus on the disciples receiving the Spirit at Pentecost, but God is just as interested in the prayer that happened during the forty days of waiting for this to happen. Waiting builds intimacy and closeness with the God of immeasurably more.

God wisely, even poetically, is writing our story within His. He teaches His children that within our wait there is purpose. It's in the waiting that we grow closer to Him.

PUSHING OUT INTO DEEPER

One day Jesus was standing on the shore of Lake Gennesaret, where a crowd had gathered to hear Him teach. This crowd were pushing around Him, so He called over two boats that were tied up at the edge of the lake. The workers in the fishing business had just come in, and were out scrubbing and repairing their nets. They brought their boats over; Jesus climbed into one of the boats and had them put out a little from the shore. He sat there and used the water and the beach as a makeshift theatre as He taught the crowd.

When His teaching was over, He turned to the head of the fishing business, a man called Simon (later to become known as Simon Peter the Rock). Jesus told Simon to "push out into deep water and let your nets out for a catch".[1]

Push out into deep water. I love that phrase, "push out". I wonder how we push out into the deeper water. Simon did it, and was amazed by what he caught. The catch of fish is an image of God's kingdom coming on earth; it was a catch of fish but it represented a catch of people. The catch is an announcement of the immeasurably more that God has for us. God doesn't just provide; He goes over the top with generosity. The catch of fish could be seen as simply a miracle involving fish, or it could be seen as a symbol of what God would do with Simon if he pushed out further into the water.

What would God do with us if we pushed out further; if we went longer and deeper in prayer? What would God do if our roots went deeper into Him?

Can we push out?

Can we press in?

Can we go closer?

Can we wait?

QUESTION: How can we show God that we're serious about having a more meaningful relationship with Him?

Immeasurably More: Small-Group Study

QUESTION: What stops you from waiting on God's presence? Can you give an honest answer rather than something like "being too busy"?

QUESTION: How patient are you? Are you able to wait for good things or do you try to make things move more quickly?

At this point, pray that as we read the passage the Holy Spirit would reveal to us what He is wanting to say through it.

READ: Isaiah 40:31 (NIV)

Then read:

Isaiah 40:27–31 (MSG)

Why would you ever complain, O Jacob,
or, whine, Israel, saying,
"God has lost track of me.
He doesn't care what happens to me"?
Don't you know anything? Haven't you been listening?
God doesn't come and go. God lasts.
He's Creator of all you can see or imagine.
He doesn't get tired out, doesn't pause to catch his breath.
And he knows everything, inside and out.
He energizes those who get tired,
gives fresh strength to dropouts.
For even young people tire and drop out,
young folk in their prime stumble and fall.
But those who wait upon God get fresh strength.
They spread their wings and soar like eagles,
They run and don't get tired,
they walk and don't lag behind.

What jumps out from this passage?

Do you notice something you haven't seen before or don't understand?

What is God saying to you in this reading?

QUESTION: What do you think is the link between waiting and the renewal of your strength?

QUESTION: What does Isaiah mean when he says that those who wait on the Lord will not be weary or feel faint? What do you think he is trying to say?

QUESTION: Why do you think God makes us wait? Could it be that He wants us to reach a place of desperation where self-sufficiency fails us?

QUESTION: What do you think opens up in us when we wait? Our hearts? Hidden places? Secret places?

QUESTION: How have you grown in faith as you have waited on God?

QUESTION: Do you think you might be able to spend more time waiting? Do you need to do anything to make this happen?

PRAY

Why don't you actively spend time waiting on God's presence? Don't try talking to Him. There is a danger that we can talk right over the top of what God is wanting to do or say to us. Find a comfortable place and simply pray, "Father, I wait on You; come and meet me," and see what happens. My tip would be, just wait longer. I often find that a more powerful wave of the Spirit is waiting around the corner, but we don't wait long enough.

---

3 FILLED, NOT SHRIVELLING

All children like grapes – I've not met one who doesn't. But not all children like raisins. That's because raisins are missing something. Juice. Grapes are raisins with all the juice still included – raisins are essentially the shrivelled version. God wants churches that are more like grapes than raisins.

We hold a service at our church once a term called "The Soak". The idea of the evening is that there is no sermon or talk but rather an extended time of worship and prayer. Many people would probably hate it, as it can seem as if there is no structure. But the truth is it's very structured. The structure is the Spirit, and we let the evening be controlled by God. As we create a time and space to wait on God, rest in His presence, and allow the Spirit to speak to and refresh us, we are able to drink of the living water that Jesus offers, so that we do not dry out or shrivel up.

Jesus is looking for a church that isn't shrivelling, but bursting with all He has to offer us.

Sadly, many of us are dead and others are shrivelled.

I once heard Ellie Mumford from the Vineyard Church speak on the work of the Holy Spirit and say that many of us are struggling to thrive because we are clinging on to religion and not a relationship. During her talk she said, "If we are here as churches for ourselves, may we shrivel."

The reality is that without the Holy Spirit and the immeasurably more that God has for us, we will indeed shrivel.

MARINATING THE MEAT

I love cooking, particularly Mexican food. The art of cooking a good Mexican dish lies in the marinating of the meat. You can't cook the meat until it has been soaked in the spices.

Marinating is the time-dependent process of soaking food in seasoning before it is cooked. It's the time element that brings about the important change. This seasoning develops and transforms the meat the longer it is left. The process can't be rushed; you can't make it go faster. It's similar to pickling the meat; it breaks down the tougher outer skin and permeates deep into the meat. The longer you marinate, the better the meat will taste.

John Arnott, an American pastor, often speaks about praying that we would be marinated in Jesus. His prayer goes:

> *May you be so marinated in the presence of the Holy Spirit, soaking in the River of God, that you no longer "taste" like your old, raw nature, but you have taken on the flavour of the Holy Spirit. "Pickle us, Lord, in the marinade of the Holy Spirit. Soak us in your wonderful presence until we become more and more like you."* [1]

While walking on water, Jesus tells Peter to join Him. Peter at this moment is willing to watch Jesus walk on water, but Jesus invites him to do more than watch and to push out, go deeper and further than he was intending to. Marinating is about saying to God, "Take me deeper; permeate my very being so that I taste and smell like You." We need to stay in the marinade (the Holy Spirit) as long as we can.

Soaking and marinating? This is all starting to sound rather strange, isn't it? Well, no. The idea of resting in God permeates right the way through the Bible. Remember that at the start of the story we were meant to rest with God in a garden.

The Lord is my shepherd, I lack nothing.
He makes me lie down in green pastures,
he leads me beside quiet waters,
he refreshes my soul.
He guides me along the right paths
for his name's sake.
Psalm 23:1–3

Be still before the Lord
and wait patiently for him;
do not fret when people succeed in
their ways,
when they carry out their wicked schemes.
Psalm 37:7

"Come to me, all you who are weary and
burdened, and I will give you rest."
Matthew 11:28–30

There remains, then, a Sabbath-rest for
the people of God; for anyone who enters
God's rest also rests from their works, just
as God did from his. Let us, therefore, make
every effort to enter that rest, so that no
one will perish by following their example of
disobedience.
Hebrews 4:9–11

He gives strength to the weary
and increases the power of the weak.
Even youths grow tired and weary,
and young men stumble and fall;
but those who hope in the Lord
will renew their strength.
They will soar on wings like eagles;
They will run and not grow weary,
they will walk and not be faint.
Isaiah 40:29–31

Before his martyrdom, an Algerian Trappist monk spoke of this fullness of God: "When You fill my heart, my eyes overflow." I want to be so full that my eyes overflow with the Spirit.

This act of soaking deeply in God's presence brings to life Acts 17:28, where it says that "in him we live and move and have our being". After all, we are human *beings*, not human doings. Soaking and marinating puts us in a position to connect with the Holy Spirit's presence in more profound ways.

SOAK

Take time now to be aware of all that God is and how He is surrounding you right now.

Marinate in the love of God.

Stop to feel His warmth, His joy.

FILLED TO THE FULL MEASURE

AND TO KNOW THIS LOVE THAT SURPASSES KNOWLEDGE – THAT YOU MAY BE FILLED TO THE MEASURE OF ALL THE FULLNESS OF GOD.
Ephesians 3:19

God wants us to be filled to the "fullness" of Him; He wants us to be fully hydrated in His Spirit. The fullness that Paul is speaking of here is a quality that is constantly replenished, refilled, and restored. God wants us to be filled and to go on being filled by His Spirit. This filling isn't a one-off event but an ongoing act. It's like a refill cup of coffee: when you've taken a sip the server comes over and tops it up to the brim. The fullness that Paul is speaking of flows from a ridiculous, lavish, and hilarious generosity.

In Ephesians 5:18 Paul uses the Greek word *pleroo*, which is translated into English as "be filled". However, the precise meaning in Greek can be understood not as just a one-off event but instead as "keeping on being filled constantly and continually".

In 2 Corinthians 9:8 (MSG) Paul writes:

> God can pour on the blessings in astonishing ways so that you're ready for anything and everything, more than just ready to do what needs to be done. As one psalmist puts it,
>
> He throws caution to the winds,
> giving to the needy in reckless abandon.
> His right-living, right-giving ways
> never run out, never wear out.
>
> This most generous God who gives seed to the farmer that becomes bread for your meals is more than extravagant with you. He gives you something you can then give away, which grows into full-formed lives, robust in God, wealthy in every way, so that you can be generous in every way, producing with us great praise to God.

Caution to the winds...
Reckless abandon...
Never runs out...
Most generous...

Do we know this as a reality in our hearts and not just an idea in our minds? God wants this to be a reality: filled to the full measure, deeper in Him, immeasurably more than we can ever imagine.

THE SPIRIT CAME UPON...

In the Bible we regularly come across the phrase "The Spirit came upon...".

The Spirit comes powerfully upon Samson[2] and he tears a lion apart with his bare hands;

The Spirit comes upon Zechariah,[3] who prophesies to the people;

The Spirit comes upon Othniel,[4] who goes to war and wins;

The Spirit comes upon Gideon[5] and he defeats the Midianite army with only 300 men;

The Spirit comes upon Mary[6] and she becomes pregnant;

The Spirit comes upon Jesus[7] and He's led into the desert before His ministry.

The Spirit came upon David, Saul, the kings, Deborah, and prophets as well as people of no real standing.

Over and over this term is used: "The Spirit came upon..." Do you believe the Spirit will come upon you? Do you believe the Spirit will come upon you to full measure, to overflowing, to hilarious overflowing?

In 1 Samuel 10 we are told that Samuel has come to anoint Saul to rule over his inheritance, land, and people. In verse 6 Samuel announces that "the Spirit of the Lord will come powerfully upon you, and you will prophesy with them; and you will be changed into a different person". When the Spirit comes upon us, we are transformed. This is the miracle of the Holy Spirit. At Pentecost, when Jesus' frightened disciples receive the Spirit, they become movement makers, revolution initiators and planet shakers. They go from being timid beginners to courageous carriers of the gospel.

The work of the Holy Spirit isn't just for the kings, rulers, or prophets of old; it's for us today. Right here, right now.

NOT JUST FOR THEN BUT FOR NOW

We can have some strange ideas about the Holy Spirit being poured out "then", for those people, but not "now", for us. We can think that the best of the Holy Spirit has already happened. But this simply isn't true, and is an outright lie of Satan himself to disarm the church of the power it has at its fingertips. If Satan can stop us finding and being continually filled by the source, he can render us powerless.

C. S. Lewis writes in *The Screwtape Letters*, **"A moderated religion is as good for us as no religion at all – and more amusing."** In this book a chief demon is training a new demon to draw someone away from the Christian faith. If the demon can convince the Christian that a moderated version of Christianity is enough, then he can render him powerless against the work of Satan. If we try to moderate the immeasurably more powerful Spirit that God has for us, then we might as well have no religion at all.

In other words, it has to be all or nothing. Without it, everything else is nothing but garbage, as Paul wrote.[8]

The truth is that the church has tried to control God for so long that we have cleverly argued that the work of the Holy Spirit was only for "then", because we don't want to make a mess by inviting Him in "now". The disciples were accused of being drunk and out of control. We don't want that in our nice, tidy churches, do we? What will the chaos of the Holy Spirit do to our neat service times, where we finish promptly in time for lunch? If we let God show up, then the liturgy would go out of the window, and what then? When would we have the sermon?!

We need to be careful that, when we say we live by the Spirit, we don't rather mean that we live by our controlled version of the Spirit.

The Bible clearly speaks of the work of the Spirit continuing.

"Don't you know that you yourselves are God's temple and that God's Spirit dwells in your midst?" (1 Corinthians 3:16)

"You, however, are not in the realm of the flesh but are in the realm of the Spirit, if indeed the Spirit of God lives in you. And if anyone does not have the Spirit of Christ, they do not belong to Christ." (Romans 8:9)

James 4:2 reminds us that "we do not have because we do not ask".

The Spirit was at work in creation, hovering over the waters, and He anointed and came upon kings and prophets. He then came at Pentecost for all people, propelling His work outwards away from the "select few" to the "select many". The Spirit moves outwards in the Gospels as more and more people experience God's presence and His power. By the time we get to Paul's writings, the work of the Spirit is apparent in towns, villages, small house churches, and individuals. People are being baptized and filled with the Spirit. Not just worthy "religious" folk but regular fishermen, carpenters, housekeepers, and farmers. Ordinary people receive the Holy Spirit with power.

Some of us might be asking how we can *know* that we are filled with the Spirit. There is a very clear danger that we regard the manifestations as proof, when some of us haven't got there yet. Peter encouragingly stands up in Jerusalem and preaches to the crowd. He shouts, "Repent and be baptized, every one of you, in the name of Jesus Christ for the forgiveness of your sins. And you will receive the gift of the Holy Spirit."[9]

Peter makes it clear that all those who repent and are baptized obtain forgiveness and receive the Spirit. If there is any doubt in your mind, simply pray and ask God to give you the Holy Spirit. God's promise is that He will give this gift to anyone who wishes to receive it. God doesn't hold it back from us.

I believe that a robust theology of the Holy Spirit leads us to believe in a truly captivating experience of God's Spirit: an experience that brings us into deeper water, an in-over-our-heads kind of experience of greater intimacy and a more effective life. God is a gentleman: He waits for our invitation. The more that God intends for us comes when we have a deeper hunger in our bellies for Him. A deeper hunger for Him and His Spirit leads us to a place of full surrender of all our ambitions, affections, desires, and possessions.

The Spirit will and does come with immeasurably more power when we yield every aspect of our life to His control. As the song goes:

> *Spirit lead me where my trust is*
> *   without borders*
> *Let me walk upon the waters*
> *Wherever You would call me*
> *Take me deeper than my feet*
> *   could ever wander*
> *And my faith will be made stronger*
> *In the presence of my Saviour*[10]
>
> **"Oceans" ("Where feet may fail"), Hillsong**

The lyrics of this Hillsong United song shape my prayer for my personal life: God, would You lead me to a place where I can fully trust You, and let me experience the deeper water where my faith will be made stronger?

> *This is my endlessly recurrent temptation: to*
> *go down to that Sea (God) and there neither*
> *dive nor swim nor float, but only dabble*
> *and splash, careful not to get out of my*
> *depth and holding on to the lifeline which*
> *connects me with my things temporal.*[11]
>
> **C. S. Lewis**

The Spirit is for today as well as yesterday, and in a little while we will look at how it is for tomorrow. But if it is true that the Spirit is for us today, now, right here, then our prayer has to be: "More, Lord; take me deeper, not to dabble or splash but to be taken out of my depth. Lord, I need more of You with and at work in me."

EPICLESIS

In my church tradition we have a word, *epiclesis*, used mostly in relation to Holy Communion. The word comes from the Ancient Greek term for "calling down from on high". When we break the bread and lift the cup, we speak of an *epiclesis* moment when the

Spirit comes down and consecrates them. We too need an *epiclesis* moment, a Spirit saturation point, a moment when we call down from on high God's empowering Spirit.

When Jesus promised the Holy Spirit, He promised it in such abundance that He said, "Whoever believes in me, as Scripture has said, rivers of living water will flow from within them" (John 7:38).

I want to encourage you to say **Yes** to the Spirit. When we say **Yes** to the Spirit we are allowing Him to take root in our lives; we're letting Him transform what He finds and empower the good news in us to become real, practical, and truly good. When we say **Yes** to the Spirit, what we find is that the fears fall away and a desperate, fearful bunch become the Jesus movement promised to the disciples. We are the church and we are God's people of good news, and He invites us to be empowered to speak boldly and act justly in all that we do.

WHY DO WE EXPECT LESS?

Why, then, are so many of us not living with this power at work in us? The truth is we are cling-ons. We are masters of clinging on to all that we think we can control. We hang on to our stuff: possessions and glittery things around us draw us away. We allow ourselves to be envious, feel guilty, worry, be discouraged, be critical, live in fear, ignore God's presence, and live in unbelief.

God wants so much more for us than being these shrivelled believers. When we are shrivelled, we expect far less than what God has to offer. We expect Him to do less, be less, and say less than He truly wants to. To receive immeasurably more from God we must let go of all the things we cling to and open ourselves up to letting go, being ridiculous, and allowing God's Spirit to free us from the fear of man and fill us to overflowing.

PRAYER

*Lord, show me what steps I can take today
to prove to You that I am serious about
getting to know You better.
Do a new and mighty work in my heart,
so that I will yearn for Your presence in
ways that will move me to action.
I don't want to be a spiritual sluggard, Lord.
I want to fulfil my God-given purpose and
potential.
Thank You that, with Your help,
I will no longer be a half-hearted Christian,
but a wholehearted servant of the Most
High God!*

AMEN.

Immeasurably More: Small-Group Study

QUESTION: How scared do you think we are of the Holy Spirit in the church? Do we fear "the mess" He might cause if He did what He did to the disciples in Acts?

QUESTION: How much is modern Christianity like that of the early church? Do you think we rely on the Holy Spirit in the same way that they did?

QUESTION: Using the metaphor of the grape and raisin, do you feel filled by the Spirit or are you shrivelling?

At this point, pray that as we read the passage the Holy Spirit would reveal to us what He is wanting to say through it.

READ: Acts 2:1–18

What jumps out from this passage?

Do you notice something you haven't seen before or don't understand?

What is God saying to you in this reading?

QUESTION: What's the link between the work of the Holy Spirit and our confidence being renewed? Have you ever experienced this yourself?

QUESTION: When the Holy Spirit was first poured out, it was very messy. People thought the disciples were drunk. Do you think the church would cope with this mess if it happened again?

QUESTION: If Pentecost happened again in this way, many would put it down to hysteria. What do you think causes fear in the church of being out of control?

QUESTION: How much do you rely on this Spirit from God? Do you behave as if it's an added extra, or an integral part of who you are?

QUESTION: James 4:2 reminds us that "We do not have because we do not ask". Do you think we ask God enough for His Spirit?

QUESTION: Are you able to imagine what the church would look like if it was strengthened daily by the Holy Spirit? How do you think it would behave?

QUESTION: Again taking the metaphor of the grape and raisin, do you think the national church is filled by the Spirit or shrivelling? Why do you think that?

QUESTION: What might your part be in seeing the church filled with both people and the Spirit? Are you able to help a small group wait upon the Lord and go from there?

PRAY

End the session by getting the group to ask God honestly for an outpouring of the Holy Spirit. Get them to pray about what makes them scared of asking for more of the Spirit, but encourage them to reveal to God their desire to be strengthened and empowered.

A Wider Story
A real story about a person called Sophie

Growing up, I was very much in the clutches of the world that surrounded me. I enjoyed the thrill of doing anything that was dangerous or wild and showed that I was uninhibited, which is what I felt. Everything was for the taking, and that excited me. I lived for the moment and didn't consider the consequences of my actions. I did have a lot of fun, and I still am tempted by the wildness of that life.

Things have changed now, though, and this temptation doesn't get the better of me any longer, as I now know what it is to live life in all its fullness as a child of God, to love and be loved, and the Spirit empowers me to resist temptations. This empowering to resist my old life has been there for nearly six years. I've never really looked back and there's no place I'd rather be than in God's presence.

Coming to faith six years ago I wanted everything that God could offer me, including the Holy Spirit and it's empowering. But, sadly, as I grew in faith I came under significant pressure to speak in tongues and "manifest" the Holy Spirit, like those around me.

At every prayer meeting, church group or small group there would come a time when someone would say, "Now let's all speak in tongues", and people would literally start using the gift of tongues all around me and I'd stand there in silence, feeling inferior, judged, and left out for not doing it. I felt like a second-rate Christian, and it broke me.

Time passed and I had to move on from that church, with love but in excitement about what was next for me. Even though I haven't felt the Holy Spirit in the way that some others have, or spoken in tongues, I am very, very confident that the Holy Spirit has been at work in me. The Spirit's hold on someone's life isn't measured by the noises they make or whether they fall over, but it's the fruit of the Spirit in their life that shows what's really going on in someone.

I've learned to seek God rather than other Christians for the Spirit. Though fellowship is helpful, it's God who gives spiritual gifts, not the church. My most amazing experiences of God's Spirit at work in me have occurred while I was with others who have never been to church. It's been while with people "doing life", when I am being the hands and feet of Jesus, that I have seen huge moves of God's Spirit.

So what has the Spirit been doing in me? **The Spirit has freed me from human condemnation, challenged me to live out my faith in the workplace, and called me to relocate onto a tough estate in East London.** The Spirit's work in me has led me to a life lived for others. Making friends with addicts and then seeing them come to faith. Making friends with neighbours and empowering them to live lives free from debt and oppression.

Have I ever felt the Spirit? No, not in the way that others speak of, such as tingles, tongues, or tumbling down, but I have experienced His power in my life, challenging and healing me and then empowering me for His work in my small area.

MOVEMENT
FOUR
WIDER

NOW TO HIM WHO IS ABLE TO DO
IMMEASURABLY MORE THAN ALL
WE ASK OR IMAGINE, ACCORDING
TO HIS POWER THAT IS **AT WORK
WITHIN US**, TO HIM BE GLORY IN
THE CHURCH AND IN CHRIST JESUS
THROUGHOUT ALL GENERATIONS.
Ephesians 3:20–21

Our fourth movement is "Wider". In previous chapters we have looked at how we gaze up at God in awe and wonder and yet realize how close this God is. Then we've looked at the importance of growing deeper roots into His presence. As we do all this we find God broadening His work in us and through us. In this section we are first going to see how God wants to widen our conception of what is possible. We will then look at the importance of being people who are "naturally supernatural" in life, and end this section by seeing that the Spirit is given not just for our enjoyment but for God's glory and renown.

1 WIDER IN US

What if God really has immeasurably more than we can even imagine? What if our imagination is simply too small, too narrow or too un-imaginative? What if God really could do more than our imagination thought possible? How would we pray differently? How audacious would our lives become? How crazy would we be willing to live in allowing ourselves to act out what this immeasurably more God had to offer the world?

Maybe we settle for immeasurably less? Maybe we make the immenseness of this brilliant God into something normal on our scale of things?

Cheryl Forbes once said: "People who live imaginative lives are 'what if' people. They relate to challenges and problems with optimism. They respond to ideas and events with a 'what if' attitude. They respond in 'what if' ways. God is a 'what if', imagination God. Here is how God works. He sees a 'formless and empty' void and asks, "what if I make a world? What if I make people in my own image? What if, when they sin I don't give up on them?"

What if God really could raise the dead?

What if God really could bring justice for the poor?

What if God really could set the captive free?

What if God really could heal the sick?

What if God really could change lives for the better?

What if God really could feed 5,000 people?

What if God really could walk on water?

What if God really could walk through walls?

What if God really could use the least significant to change the world?

What if God really could transform broken marriages?

What if God really could set people free from addictions?

What if God really could be born of a virgin?

What if God really could raise Himself from the dead?

What if all of that was only the start?

> IF THE HOLY SPIRIT SHOULD COME AGAIN UPON US AS IN EARLIER TIMES, VISITING CHURCH CONGREGATIONS WITH THE SWEET BUT FIERY BREATH OF PENTECOST, WE WOULD BE GREATER CHRISTIANS AND HOLIER SOULS. BEYOND THAT, WE WOULD ALSO BE GREATER POETS AND GREATER ARTISTS AND GREATER LOVERS OF GOD AND OF HIS UNIVERSE.
>
> **A. W. Tozer**

Jesus wants all of us to live a radically powerful life. He gives us the strength to do far more with Him than we could possibly do without Him. Despite all the ways in which we try to define and control Him, Jesus reminds us that He has immeasurably more to offer us, our families, friends, and neighbourhoods than simply a religious life.

GLORIOUSLY RUINED

God is wanting to give us the beautiful gift of the Spirit to empower our lives for radical living for Him. Some of us will feel and recognize that we are open to the work of the Holy Spirit, while others will be aware of being closed. Closed people start with the presumption that nothing will happen either in church or in the workplace that is out of the normal rhythm of life. Closed people believe that faith is nothing but a choice based on facts, and that faith in Jesus is primarily about getting through life so we can get to the good stuff after death.

Open people begin by believing that there is more available, and they are filled with expectancy that God is doing something new today and that if they are open to it they might sense, see, or experience God as present right now.

It is possible to be a closed person and not even realize it, thinking that you're open to God when actually you're not. Just because you believe in Jesus and attend church doesn't mean you are open. It just means you're looking in the right place.

In the same way, you might assume you are closed, but have never really thought much about it. Yet despite not thinking about and reacting to the Holy Spirit, you might find that you have been filled all along, and just didn't know it.

We can think we are open but actually be fearful of what that means, so we hold on to what we know, hold on to what is present to us: work, busyness, and the reality of the physical. We hold on to our logic and we hold on to our senses. We may not realize it but we put parameters around ourselves to protect us. We protect the dream of health, wealth, and happiness, all the while failing to realize that this dream we are clinging on to will ruin us and lead us away from God's immeasurably more.

Clinging on to our own hopes, dreams, wealth, and happiness keeps God's hopes, dreams, and presence at arm's length.

We do this either to protect ourselves and our desire to remain in control, arguing "This is my life", or to protect our public image by not wanting to look foolish, like the disciples in Acts 2. Or we think we're protecting God from what He will not do even if we ask Him. By not engaging with the Spirit we can protect ourselves from the idea that God doesn't want to use us. In fear we can think we are open while actually we are locked down, clamped up, surrounded by a ten-foot wall of control.

Lucy, a little girl in C. S. Lewis's *Chronicles of Narnia*, is overwhelmed by the awesome magnificence of Aslan the lion. For those who have never read them, Aslan is the mysterious and powerful lion who represents God in the Narnia tales. In response to hearing about Aslan, Lucy asks, "Is he safe?" The reply she gets is, "No, he is not safe, but he is good."

Being open to God and the immeasurably greater work of His Spirit isn't safe. How could it be?

But it *is* good.

Jesus wants us to be *gloriously ruined* by His dangerous Spirit. Jesus wants us to be open, not closed as we often are. God asks us to make a dangerous surrender because He is powerful and good. He wants us to yield our sense of personal power, wisdom, and strength and become open to Him.

The truth of life is that we can be ruined by what we hold on to, but I want to be ruined by something that will last.

BEFORE WE RUSH ON – DISAPPOINTMENTS

It is important for us to pause for a moment and admit to something that might be welling up inside us at this point. There is a danger that our disappointments might have a greater effect on our imagination than we would like to think. We're talking about God having a wider work in and through us, but many of us will be frozen in our own soul. We have heard people speak of this "more" that God has for us but we are locked in a place of disappointment that is crippling us for the future work God plans for us.

I recently asked a group of Christians, "Who in the room is a little disappointed with God?" Hands shot up all over the place. You could feel a gasp of breath as people around the room had that "me too!" moment. We aren't the only ones to be disappointed; we have all secretly (and some not so secretly) carried this disappointment in our hearts, making us a little bitter, jaded, or cynical.

We need to be a "real" church, where we can speak about disappointment, mental health, anxiety, and depression. A church that doesn't brush tough issues under the carpet. There has to be a way for us that is so beautifully Jesus-like that it can hold the heartache and the expectancy of the resurrection in tension. Jesus clearly had to die before He could be resurrected, but it is noticeable that too often we rush to the triumph of Easter Sunday while trying to skip past the sadness of Good Friday. We need to be a church with high hopes and high expectations while at the same time not ignoring the pain and rejection felt when something hasn't worked out.

I want to focus on the wider work of God, but need to be honest about the reality of disappointment. In fact, in Movement Five: Further, there is a whole section on disappointment. So you will need to wait or jump ahead to read more! I believe in the wider work of God but at the same time I struggle with unanswered prayer. As we spend this next Movement looking at the wider work of God's Spirit, can we hold this in tension with our disappointments? There is a danger that our disappointments in fact imprison us in fear. We ask ourselves, "What if I pray for a miracle and nothing happens?" So we don't pray, in case we are disappointed.

Sometimes our disappointments can be down to a lack of faith that God is even capable. Essentially, the question for us is, "Does God care?" If He does in fact care, then we can ask, "Do we really trust Him?" If God doesn't care then we can't trust Him, but if He does care then surely we can trust Him.

The reality is that rather than focusing on the WIDER work of the Holy Spirit we focus on the storm, mountain, or catastrophe before us. We see the problem as bigger than the God of more. This can and will cripple us, as it tells us that God isn't as powerful as we hoped or dreamed. God isn't able or capable. May I suggest that we dare to hold our disappointment and cynicism while at the same time having a growing sense of anticipation of something God could be doing?

As David reminds us time and time again in the Psalms, there is only one way of shifting this crippling overload of fear, anxiety, worry, and disappointment.

One moment in Psalm 77 David cries out, "Will the Lord reject for ever? Will he never show his favour again?[1] But the next minute he is worshipping: "Your ways, God, are holy. What god is as great as our God? You are the God who performs miracles; you display your power among the peoples."[2]

The Bible is honest about the fact that disappointment and worship journey side by side.

Are you able to list your disappointments in God?

i.

ii.

iii.

iv.

v.

QUESTION: How have these disappointments stopped you praying for further things?

QUESTION: Do you think you might be able to hold your disappointments in one hand while on the other having a growing sense of anticipation of what you might be praying for?

THE KISS

Many of us who are married would say that we remember the first time we kissed our wife or husband. It might be memorable because it went wrong (clashing of teeth, far too wet...) or because it was so good. Some of us will remember it because of where it happened or because it was unexpected. The truth about such a kiss is that if we only ever got that one kiss we would be happy because of who we were with. It would still be memorable. But the good news is that it wasn't the only kiss; there were others that followed. This first kiss probably wasn't the best of all the kisses, but it was the most memorable and was a sign of greater things to follow.

Like this kiss, the Holy Spirit at Pentecost was the first fruit of a harvest still to come. To comprehend the work of the Holy Spirit we first need to understand why it came at Pentecost, which fell on the Jewish harvest festival. It wasn't simply that the Holy Spirit's entrance happened to coincide with that festival. Bad timing, and sorry for the clash! But the arrival of the Holy Spirit can be understood in the light of the day it occurred.

We are told in Acts 2 that the day of Pentecost had come. It is like saying Christmas Day had arrived; people would have been counting down to that day. The day of Pentecost was keenly anticipated because it was the festival of Shavuot, or first fruits. This festival was a big deal for all those who tended land or produced crops. The harvest festival didn't occur at the end of the harvest, to celebrate all that had been grown; it came at the start, to celebrate all that was still to come. The festival of Shavuot was a day when all the Jews would congregate in the city of Jerusalem with the "first fruits" of their harvests: grain, lambs, drink and food offerings. If you grew it, then you would take the first of that crop in the belief that this wasn't all you would receive, but that if you offered it to God with a thankful heart the harvest would be multiplied. This was a festival of living in hope of more to come.

This festival was about the beginning of a new harvest, a new season, and a new year of produce. It wasn't by chance that God chose this day; it was deliberately picked to send a deeper message. The disciples speaking in other languages, flames over heads, wind gushing around small rooms, and 3,000 coming to faith is nothing but the "first fruits" of what God has to offer. What the people experienced on that day was the start of a new season. This wasn't going to be a one-off event but one that inaugurated a new season of the Holy Spirit's work.

The Holy Spirit until this point had been given to individuals at specific times. At Pentecost the work of the Spirit suddenly broadened out to include all people. Not just those in kingly authority or those with a prophetic message, but all people could now experience and receive it. Pentecost is the signal that God's work extends far beyond our ill-thought-out boundaries.

We need to have a Pentecost imagination for the work of the Spirit. Until this point, the disciples wouldn't have been able to imagine what the work of the Holy Spirit would be like. Their minds wouldn't have enabled them to picture what could happen, as there was little to base it on. The reality is that we shrink our imagination because we don't want to be disappointed, so in fear we step back and limit our dreams.

MASENO

A number of years ago I was a part of a mission team sent to Maseno in Kenya. A group of friends and I run a farm school out there, helping orphans to grow crops and educating them in farming techniques. We had taken around ten young people out to see the project but also to encourage them to move outside their comfort zones. What I didn't realize was that *my* comfort zone would also be stretched.

I'd first experienced the healing work of the Holy Spirit for myself when at university. I had broken my collarbone while playing squash and I'd tried to manage it for a few weeks. Eventually I had ended up in A&E in excruciating pain after bumping it yet again. The X-ray showed a break in the bone and the two sections of bone misaligned, with a nerve trapped between them. I was promised an operation to try to realign the bone and was told to return the following Monday. I left with an arm strapped up and a lump growing on my collarbone. This lump I described as an egg on my shoulder, and I still have it today. That Sunday night I turned up at church and during the worship towards the end of the service Dave the pastor stood up and announced that God wanted to heal someone with an egg on their shoulder. This rather shocked me, as nobody at the church was aware of what I had done or of the name I was calling my lump. I eventually went forward for prayer and two teenage boys were assigned to pray for me. They told me that I was their first, as they had been trained only that afternoon. My heart sank: I had the rookies! What was the point? I wanted the experienced and knowledgable prayer warriors, those with a good string of Christian cliché phrases to make the prayers sound more holy. Yet after some moments of prayer my shoulder became hot and dripped with sweat, and the pain slipped away. I went home praising God that the pain had gone. When I returned to the hospital on the Monday morning an X-ray showed that the break was gone and the bone had been healed.

So I believed in healing. I'd experienced it myself, but I hadn't experienced quite what I went on to see one afternoon in Aqwanda village, Kenya. In that one afternoon, ten teenagers and I saw over sixty healings. People arrived at the small rural church with bad backs, injured legs, blindness, deafness, and many headaches. That afternoon we saw blind old farmwomen receive sight, lame farm workers walk away with no sticks, and children regain hearing.

But it was the girl with the burn scab that rocked my imagination. I joined an eighteen-year-old girl to pray for a nine-year-old girl who had fallen over a fire and had a burn on her ankle the size of a tennis ball. I encouraged the older girl to pray for the scab. She placed her hand over it and prayed that the little girl would be healed. As she took away her hand, we noticed that the scab was significantly smaller; it was now around two-thirds of its original size. We prayed again, covering the mark with her hand, and when she removed it, it was now the size of a ping-pong ball. We kept praying again and again until it was the size of a small fingernail.

The box that I had shut God in needed upgrading, because this left me gobsmacked. Seeing something like this happen with my own eyes sent my imagination reeling.

Let's look at what this means for us, before we turn to what it means for others.

ME

Ephesians 3 says that God will do immeasurably more than all we ask or think[3] or imagine,[4] according to His power at work within us. This means that our personal expectations need to shift. We've talked before about a sense of wonder; well, this sense of wonder needs to broaden our desire to see more happen around us.

1. WIDER ASKING

Some years ago when I was at theological college training for ministry, we were in a lecture about prayer. We were asked to get into groups and pray together and listen to the words we used. We had to keep our ears open to the language used and see if there were any repeated words.

One word kept coming up in poorly thought-through sentences and started to grate on us. We realized that maybe sometimes, unintentionally, what we were asking of God was rather narrow. Time after time we used the word "just" when asking for things: "Father, would You 'just' be involved in..."; "Lord, we 'just' pray that..." Did we really only want God to do just this one thing? Surely we want God to do many wonderful and brilliant things! Ever since then my ears have been alert for the word "just". We have a God of immeasurably more, not a God of immeasurably less. We need to be careful that what we desire and ask for isn't much less than what God has to offer. We need to be asking big, bold, wild prayers. We need to be asking for the unimaginable.

We need to dare to pray for what isn't possible because we believe in a God of endless possibilities.

2. WIDER THINKING

Some translations of the passage in Ephesians 3, such as the NIV, don't have the word "think". This is another of those problems with the translation from Greek to English. The word used, *noeo*, can be translated as "think" or "imagine" or "understand". But the transforming of our thinking is the key to what Paul wants for the church. The disciples thought that a man couldn't walk on water, but he did. The disciples believed a man couldn't walk through solid walls, but Jesus did. If we are going to see the world transformed, renewed, and healed, then our minds need to be transformed first. We need to review what we consider to be possible. Our minds try to limit our thoughts about what is possible. We create boundaries to how the world works: rules for the universe.

The disciples thought that a man couldn't rise from the dead. That's why they went back to their old business of fishing. They thought it was all over, but the truth is that it was only the beginning. We narrow our understanding of the universe; we believe that our tomorrows will be the same as today. But the resurrection reminds us that what was dead today could be alive tomorrow. We need to renew our minds and reconsider what we think the God of immeasurably more is capable of.

3. WIDER IMAGINING

Imagining what is possible involves going beyond what we think is possible to dreaming of what can become possible once Jesus sets before us a new, different landscape – one that opens up before us and starts to redeem our imagination.

Walter Brueggemann comments as follows:

> *What the church does with its creeds and its doctrinal tradition, **it flattens out all the images and metaphors to make it fit into a nice little formulation and then it's deathly** [emphasis mine]. So we have to communicate to people, if you want a God that is healthier than that, you're going to have to take time to sit with these images and relish them and let them become a part of your prayer life and your vocabulary and your conceptual frame. Which, again, is why the poetry is so important because the poetry just keeps opening and opening and opening whereas the doctrinal practice of the church is always to close and close and close until you're left with nothing that has any transformative power.*[5]

It is the Holy Spirit at work in us that becomes the inspirer of human imagination. It's this Spirit that gives us a wide, extensive sphere of action and possibility. It is the wider work of the Spirit in us, a life transformed by the Spirit, that gives us a new imagination that is the imagination of the prophet.

> *We need to ask not whether it is realistic or practical or viable but whether it is imaginable. We need to ask if our consciousness and imagination have been so assaulted and co-opted by the royal consciousness that we have been robbed of the courage or power to think an alternative thought.*[6]
> **Walter Brueggemann**

Walter Brueggemann argues here that we need a new "Prophetic Imagination". This prophetic imagination is going to be possible only because of the presence of the Spirit in us and the rebirth of our minds.

We need a wider conception of what God is able to do in us. The power of the Holy Spirit in us and for us is immeasurably more than we can imagine.

> *There must be more than this;*
> *O breath of God, come breathe within...*[7]
> **Tim Hughes, "Consuming Fire"**

God has more for you than you can imagine. He has more for you to receive, experience, and be. When we think we understand God we need to be reminded there is more of God to see, there is more of God to experience, and more of God's transforming Spirit to remake us.

TO SEE A WIDER WORK

To see a wider work of God in us and through us, we must not focus on the overwhelming task, miracle, or mountain ahead of us but through worship and prayer focus on the HIGHER God before us. In prayer and worship we are able to give to God all these fears that cripple and hinder us. It's in worship that we glance HIGHER than we have been able to before, and recognize the glorious power that our Creator has over the whole of creation. He is powerful in our disappointments and has authority over our heartache.

The questions for us to ask ourselves are things like...

Do I believe that our prayers will and can make a difference in our lives and the lives of those we love?

Do I believe that our prayers have the power to change things?

Do I believe that God is ultimately good, graceful, and all-powerful?

Recently a really good friend has found himself praying desperately for a loved one who is critically ill. While praying and worshipping one night he found himself crying out to God, asking why he wasn't seeing the breakthrough he was wanting. God's WIDER work wasn't apparent to him. Crying out in prayer, he heard God speak to him...

I'm here, I love you, and I have a plan.

We don't always know why things don't work out the way we want. I'm not sure we are *meant* to understand. Sometimes in the untangling of a desperate situation all we hear are the gentle words *I'm here, I love you, and I have a plan.*

I don't see this as a failure on God's part but as a strengthening of our faith, enabling us to trust and to wake each day with a renewed excitement about all that the God of immeasurably more has for us, while at the same time admitting our disappointments.

The resurrection is a daily reminder that what we think we know about how the world works, how we understand its nature, and the rules it plays by, are in fact a lie and that much more is possible than we can ever dream or envisage. If we are going to make

Jesus **HIGHER**, become **CLOSER** to Him, and go **DEEPER** into His presence, then He certainly wants to see Himself spreading **WIDER** in us. "Wider" is the radical transforming Spirit's work in our lives. Jesus doesn't want the Spirit to have a narrow work but a broad and transforming one. This wider work for some of us might mean first healing past hurts, disappointments, regrets, and heartache to enable something new to be born.

Because of the "deeper" God in us, we are now called to a radically wider life in response. A wider life is a life full of wonder and anticipation at what is possible. If God truly is higher than we can imagine, then our eyes should always be open, expecting to see something new and wonderful happening.

Immeasurably More: Small-Group Study

QUESTION: How do you think modern Western Christians might have narrowed our understanding of God?

QUESTION: The early church was radically empowered by the Holy Spirit and saw wonderful miracles, including people coming back from the dead. How desperate do you think the church is at the moment for these outworkings of God's kingdom?

QUESTION: Why do you think this is the case?

At this point, pray that as we read the passage the Holy Spirit would reveal to us what He is wanting to say through it.

READ: Ephesians 3:20–21

What jumps out from this passage?

Do you notice something you haven't seen before or don't understand?

What is God saying to you in this reading?

QUESTION: Paul writes in Ephesians that God is able to do much more than our minds can ask for or imagine. My imagination is rather vivid. This must mean that God is something special. What does this tell you about God?

QUESTION: Where has your imagination been limited in the past with regard to God?

QUESTION: If God can do immeasurably more than we can ask or imagine, why do you think we constantly shrink our imagination? Is it because of fear? Our own ego? Our wanting to be self-sufficient? Could it be because it's easier for us not to need to build a relationship with the source of this "more"?

QUESTION: Paul says this "more" in Jesus is for people throughout all the generations. Do you think we have a tendency to see miracles as something from times gone by? If so, why do you think this?

QUESTION: Where do you think your personal expectations need a shift with regard to what God is capable of doing?

QUESTION: Sometimes it's through unanswered prayer that our expectations shrink. Are you able to express how unanswered prayer might have hampered your desire to pray for future miracles?

QUESTION: What do you think Paul means by "to him be glory in the church"?

PRAY

God, You can do anything; You know far more than we could ever imagine or guess or request even in our wildest dreams! You do it not by pushing us around but by working within us, by Your Spirit deeply and gently within us.

Glory to God in the church!
Glory to God in the Messiah, in Jesus!
Glory down all the generations!
Glory through all millennia!

Oh, yes![8]

Amen.

GOD IS ABLE TO DO MORE THAN
MAN CAN UNDERSTAND.

Thomas à Kempis, *Imitation of Christ*

2 NATURALLY SUPERNATURAL

THE GOOD NEWS OF THE KINGDOM
MESSAGE OF JESUS IS THIS: THAT
WITH HIS COMING, THE RULE OF
GOD'S LOVE IS NOW WITHIN THE
REACH OF ANYONE WHO WILL
TURN AND COMMIT TO HIM. THEY
CAN ALL "TASTE.... THE POWER OF
THE AGE TO COME" (HEBREWS 6:5).[1]

We all have ideas about what is natural and normal. Yet science tells us there is no such thing as normal. The universe bends and contorts: rules of light and time get twisted at the end of the universe. What we call normal is only what we perceive to be normal. What we see as normal most probably isn't what the disciples thought was normal after they received the Holy Spirit. After you have seen fish ripping your nets and a man walk on water and then through a wall, when you have seen men raised from the dead and the blind get their sight, I bet your sense of "normal" is challenged.

What we call normal is normal only to us. If you were to travel to another country, its rules would be different from your country's. What you can get away with here might be illegal in another state. What we call normal behaviour here may well be abnormal there. As Karl Pilkington says in his TV travel show *The Moaning of Life*, "Who's the mental one here? Is it me or everyone else?"

We need to be very careful when we talk about what is normal, standard, and ordinary. Maybe God's ordinary is twelve miracles before breakfast...

Pause for a moment and take stock of this. For Jesus, the resurrection wasn't a miracle, but part of how God always meant the world to work. In God's economy, miracles aren't miracles... They are just what God does before breakfast. They are simply what's natural and normal in the world He created. Although they are "normal" to God, they are still something to make us stop and take notice, so we do want to expect them, but we don't want to regard them as being so normal that we lose the wonder that we spoke of earlier, which points us to the glory of God.

What is a miracle? A miracle is something that we perceive to be impossible within our understanding of the world, but which by God's grace occurs anyway. A miracle is an incident that is not possible according to human power or will or the laws of nature, and consequently is attributed to a supernatural, especially divine, being. These unexplained happenings are often attributed to a miracle worker, saint, or religious leader. Miracles aren't possible in our laws of nature.

But maybe we are living in a cul-de-sac, closed off and unaware of what is going on at the end of the road.

Maybe we need to leave our Christian cul-de-sac and enter the wider road? A wider road where what we think is normal is turned upside down and the new normal includes miracles done by God.

A PENTECOST PEOPLE

We need to reclaim the title "Pentecost People", which is often associated with the Pentecostal Church. The Pentecostal Church does not own or even claim to hold captive the Holy Spirit. We need in our minds to take back the Holy Spirit; it's for all of us. We are all becoming Pentecost People. As we allow the work of the Holy Spirit to redefine our imagination, we develop a wider expectation of what is possible. The gifts of the Spirit are given to fulfil this vision. As Pentecost People we are realizing that the work of the early church is also available to today's church. But, because of years of fear and the devil undermining who we are in Christ, we end up unsure, unclear, and well out of our comfort zones. We start to think that natural and normal means struggling, and that God's economy is nothing but myth and fairy tale.

Over time, we have a tendency to lean away from the supernatural and so each generation needs to lean back into God. Our default is towards familiarity and laziness. We need to be leaning in the opposite direction to that in which our heart so easily pushes us. We need to lean into Pentecost again and again.

Pentecost People live with an expectation that God will do something, even if it's not what we imagine. God will do something because He promises to give us what we ask for. Jesus teaches the disciples, "Keep on asking, and you will receive what you ask for. Keep on seeking, and you will find. Keep on knocking, and the door will be opened to you."[2]

Jesus calls us to a radical, empowered existence if and as we respond to the deeper life that He has for us.

ACCESS ALL AREAS

A friend of mine plays in a well-known band in the charts and every now and again we get tickets to go to see them in concert. The tickets we get say ACCESS ALL AREAS, which means we get to go backstage after the gig and meet the band. Getting tickets to see a band or a performance is exciting, but having an ACCESS ALL AREAS pass is the real deal. This kind of ticket lets us walk around the back of the stage without being asked where we are going.

God wants an ACCESS ALL AREAS pass to our hearts and lives. Being a Pentecost People means allowing God to move freely in our hearts, wherever He wants to go.

The question is: What is stopping us from experiencing this?

What are we scared of losing in order to gain all that God has for us?

DEAD BODIES

As part of my job, I have to lead people's funerals. It's such a privilege to be able to help a family say goodbye to a loved one. Imagine that one day I'm taking a funeral and nobody shows up. All I have is the body of the deceased, and the funeral is cancelled. For some strange reason I bring the body home for safekeeping and I prop it up in my living room, giving it the most comfy chair we have.

Imagine, then, that my wife walks into the living room and asks what I am doing. I tell her that I have John Doe in the lounge. I tell her that John Doe is a good man who lives on the estate where we live and that he loves to spend time with his friends and family. What I have said is partly true. There is a body in our lounge; it has limbs, eyes, a mouth, hands, and feet. But the truth is that it is a body that is missing something. It's less than half of what it should be. It's missing a heartbeat.

Why is it that the church often can feel as if it's missing something? It has limbs, and eyes, and mouths, hands, and feet. The body of Christ is present but there is still something missing. Maybe it's missing the heartbeat.

R. T. Kendall opens his book on the Holy Spirit by saying:

> *One of the most frightening comments I have heard since I entered the ministry was uttered by an Episcopalian priest in America: "IF the Holy Spirit were taken completely from the church, 90 per cent of the work of the church would go right on as if nothing had happened!" What a travesty of what the church was meant to be! And can it be true also of our personal lives – that many of us are churning out "Christian" activity that has no touch of God upon it?*[3]

The Holy Spirit gives the church its heartbeat. We can have all the parts of a body but still be missing something: the heartbeat, the engine room.

The church cannot be quite what it could be or what it's meant to be. The church can be a body or it can be a Pentecost People.

Jesus realized that it was possible to be physically alive and at the same time dead. A number of times in the Gospels He claims that people can have a physical heartbeat but be spiritually dead. I have to be very careful here, because there is no mention in the Gospels of Jesus ever separating out our spiritual life and our physical life. Everything is spiritual when it comes to Jesus. Everything is naturally spiritual. As Jackie Pullinger said, "To the spiritual person the supernatural seems natural."[4]

But there are a number of times in the Gospels when Jesus speaks of dead people walking.

At the end of the story of the prodigal son, the father turns to the older son, who has never left home, stating, "Your brother was dead and now is alive again."

The boy was dead and is now alive. Something has changed.

In Luke 9 we have another story. Jesus is walking down the road when a young man comes to Him proclaiming his desire to follow Him wherever He goes. Jesus tells him to follow but the young man says he needs to go back and help bury his father. Jesus turns to him and says, "Let the dead bury the dead."

Have you ever seen a zombie burying a zombie?

No. Then Jesus must be talking about something else, right?

Correct. Jesus makes the presumption that although we might be carrying a pulse, there is another part of us that is dead. If you have ever sat with someone who is a heroin addict you will notice that they are physically alive, but there is a deadness inside them.

They are alive and dead at the same time.

Jesus in His death and resurrection and then the outpouring of the Holy Spirit brings our two halves together. We become both physically alive and spiritually alive. We become naturally something new... naturally supernatural.

Imagine

Imagine a car with no engine; imagine a church without power.

The reality is that we don't need to imagine too much, as we see it all too often. The question for us is: What kind of church are we dreaming of?

A church that is stagnant and uninspired or a church that is living and breathing, connected to the engine? Going somewhere and doing something. The revolution of Jesus cannot happen without the empowering of the Holy Spirit.

QUESTION: What would the church look like to you if it was connected perfectly to the power source?

ACTS

The book of Acts is the story of the *action* of the Holy Spirit. If the Gospels are about Jesus and His work, then the book of Action (Acts) is the story of the Holy Spirit spilling out, drenching the people, and drowning them in life. As we plot the story of the book of Action we see the Holy Spirit spiralling out from the epicentre of Jerusalem. Essentially, the Spirit coming at Pentecost is a symbol of first fruits but also an announcement that the religious epicentre of the Jewish faith is itself being renewed. The Holy Spirit is poured out over a city and the city sees thousands coming to faith. Religion is being left behind for a new life-giving relationship.

LET'S PLOT THE STORY OF THE BOOK OF ACTION

Acts 1 – A scared bunch of apprentices are in hiding. Scared for their lives, they WAIT for God to do what He has promised.

Acts 2 – The day of the outpouring comes and they are transformed. This bunch of nervous men and women are given a power that leaves them clear of mind, at peace, energized, excited, and with authority to pray for healing, preach with confidence, and lead people to faith.

Peter stands to give his first sermon and clearly preaches the gospel of grace. During the sermon he quotes from Joel 2:

> *In the last days, God says,*
> *I will pour out my Spirit on all people.*
> *Your sons and daughters will prophesy,*
> *your young men will see visions,*
> *your old men will dream dreams.*
> *Even on my servants, both men and women,*
> *I will pour out my Spirit in those days,*
> *and they will prophesy.*
> *I will show wonders in the heavens above*
> *and signs on the earth below,*

blood and fire and billows of smoke.
The sun will be turned to darkness
and the moon to blood
before the coming of the great and glorious
day of the Lord.
And everyone who calls
on the name of the Lord will be saved.

Peter concludes with: "Repent and be baptized... And you will receive the gift of the Holy Spirit." And if there is any question in our minds about whether this outpouring is still available to us today, Peter also says, "The promise is for you and your children and for all who are far off – for all whom the Lord our God will call."

This promise of Joel was a promise for the disciples, a promise for the early church, and a promise for YOU.

On hearing this, 3,000 people said yes. The work of the Holy Spirit brings about miracles. My coming to faith is one of those God-natural miracles; there is no human reason why I would choose to know Jesus. It's a miracle that He found me and a miracle that He saved me. The same was true for the 3,000 who came to faith that day. Salvation and evangelism are the work of the Holy Spirit.

The work of the Holy Spirit has a central role in the church. Acts 2 tells us that it's a key and prominent feature of the church. Before the Spirit, the church wasn't the church; it was just a bunch of scared people. If we hop through the book of Acts we can see key moments where the Spirit is at work.

Acts 3 – It's just another day in the life of these naturally supernatural Pentecost People. Peter and John are at the Beautiful gate in Jerusalem. They are heading to the Temple as they have done many times before, but this time they are interrupted by a lame beggar. Peter takes him by the right hand and in a moment this man who has been a cripple all his life stands up and walks. Well, runs, skips, and jumps.

Acts 4 – The church members are under pressure and find themselves being challenged by the religious institutions. Anxious, they gather together and pray for boldness. After they have prayed together, we are told that "the place where they were meeting was shaken. And they were all filled with the Holy Spirit and spoke the word of God boldly."

They are receiving more of the Spirit; it wasn't a one-off event. They pray for more, and more comes. New waves of the Spirit hit the church. They are empowered again; more people receive, and they speak boldly again.

Acts 8 – Jerusalem is being transformed. The church is being pressed on every side but people keep coming to faith, including a magician and sorcerer called Simon. Simon was the David Blaine or Dynamo of Jerusalem. He did amazing magic tricks and people thought he was incredible – so incredible that they called him the "Great Power"; many thought he was a messiah. Simon hears the gospel and comes to faith but then stumbles and asks if he is able to buy the gift of the Holy Spirit. Already people are trying to control the divine. The religious behaviour of working, purchasing, or manipulating God is back on the scene.

Acts 10 – Peter has visions that renew the church's understanding of the holiness code. Peter's revelation goes on to transform old thinking into new thinking.

Acts 13 – The Holy Spirit speaks to the church during a prayer and worship time, telling the people to send Paul and Barnabas out to do the work that He has anointed them for. This anointing is for a purpose: not for the church's edification but so the world might hear and see the kingdom.

Acts 14–28 becomes the story of the Spirit moving out into Cyprus, Iconium, Lystra and Derbe, Antioch, Macedonia, Thessalonica, Berea, Corinth, Ephesus, through Macedonia and Greece, and then on to Rome itself. The Holy Spirit is present throughout this adventure.

God's plan was never that Jesus would come, show us what was possible, die and be resurrected, and then leave us to it. The plan was always that we would need help to carry out His mission. Our problem is that we don't recognize the scale of the help He is offering and making available to us.

In the book of Acts the church starts to see the world through God's eyes. They start to see what's possible when the Spirit is hovering over the waters. In Acts, scales fall from Paul's eyes and he sees the world anew. We need the scales of our spiritual blindness to fall away so that we can see the world as the place it really is: a place where heaven and earth are starting to collide. We need to see the thin places where the two worlds are blending into each other. We need to see the world of earthly natural and the world of kingdom natural merging together to create something beautifully new.

NATURALLY SUPER

God's plan for His church is that we would become naturals in the works, signs, and wonders of His kingdom on earth. The church is to be an empowered group of people who have the confidence to step out and pray for the things the world would say aren't possible. But what does this mean? What should we actually be doing? If we look back, the Scriptures show us the kinds of things that God has done through His people before: oceans were split in two, eyes were opened, the lame walked, dead people were raised, and for a moment a man walked on water.

The Bible is full of moments in which the divide between heaven and earth is wafer-thin. We must conclude that these things were right for then and that some of them might be right for us now. If Pentecost was the first fruits, then we must ask what God wants from us today. Could He have more planned? Let's not think narrowly that the old miracles are the only ones available today. Might we have bigger and more incredible things to do? Could we dare to pray for them?

> *It is perfectly clear that in New Testament times, the gospel was authenticated in this way by signs, wonders and miracles of various characters and descriptions... Was it only meant to be true of the early church? ... The Scriptures never anywhere say that these things were only temporary – never! There is no such statement anywhere.*[5]

God has immeasurably more for us in our very understanding of our identity. We aren't just to be people who believe, but also people who act out this kingdom He is bringing closer to earth. In Matthew 10:8 (ESV) Jesus commissions His followers and says, "Proclaim as you go, saying, 'The kingdom of heaven is at hand.' Heal the sick, raise the dead, cleanse lepers, cast out demons."

Jesus commissions the disciples and later in Matthew tells them to hand on this work from one generation to the next. Had you ever thought that God might want you to do one of these works? Healing the sick? Raising the dead? Cleansing the unclean? Casting out the demonic?

The modern church is commissioned and called to the same work, by the same Spirit, as the early church. An authentic Jesus life is a life free from our sin, alive in the Spirit to implement this kingdom call.

My deep conviction is that God wants His church to be as empowered and victorious as it was 2,000 years ago. **Jesus wants a church that is courageously empowered to share the good news and see lives transformed.** Not just in terms of an idea of the good news but in terms of a life changed and healed. It's this naturally supernatural church that can share the good news, not just in a head-to-head conversion but in a heart conversion. It is the power of the Spirit that can touch hearts.

The question facing us in any situation would be: If Jesus were here, would He pray for a miracle, and should we thus dare to do the same?

Immeasurably More: Small-Group Study

QUESTION: Do you think that being supernatural people is natural for us or abnormal?

QUESTION: Do you agree or disagree with this statement: "The Holy Spirit gives the church its heartbeat. We can have all the parts of a body but still be missing something: the heartbeat, the engine room"?

At this point, pray that as we read the passage the Holy Spirit would reveal to us what He is wanting to say through it.

READ: Acts 3:1–10

What jumps out from this passage?

Do you notice something you haven't seen before or don't understand?

What is God saying to you in this reading?

QUESTION: What significance do you think the time of day has in the passage? The number three reminds us of the resurrection on the third day. Is the writer trying to tell us something?

QUESTION: The prayer prayed is rather simple: "In the name of Jesus Christ of Nazareth, walk." Why do you think this is?

QUESTION: The story seems to oversimplify prayer ministry, with no need for lots of waiting or praying. Can prayer for healing really be this simple?

QUESTION: Has anyone experienced prayer for healing and seen an answer this quickly, or heard stories of it?

QUESTION: Why does Peter pray in the name of Jesus? What's the significance of this?

QUESTION: Missionary and author Jackie Pullinger said, "To the spiritual person the supernatural seems natural." Do you think God intended us to be involved naturally with His miracles on a daily basis?

QUESTION: We can often want to make excuses for why we don't see miracles every day. Do you think the problem is with God or with us?

QUESTION: Do you think it's possible for the church to exist and yet be dead to what God has for it?

QUESTION: Have you ever had the courage to pray for a miracle or to see something wonderful happen? What happened? Try to spot even the smallest miracles in your story. These can raise your faith level.

PRAY

Spend some time in prayer, asking God to show you what a naturally supernatural life looks like. Ask for courage to pray more for miracles, signs, and wonders of the kingdom. Ask God to work through your unbelief to bring about a stronger sense of what He has created for you to do.

---

3 WIDER FOR THE WORLD

My wife, like many people, loves to spend a day at a spa. She returns feeling relaxed, chilled out, and soothed from all the stresses and strains of life. A day at a spa is beautifully relaxing, as you feel the pressures of life lift off you.

Sadly, we behave as if the church is a spiritual spa. We attend services, spend time with God, and even receive His Holy Spirit and come away feeling chilled. Sometimes during our evening service God really shows up (whatever that means), and we spend the time really resting in His presence. It feels great; we come away refreshed and encouraged.

Sometimes we behave as if this time with God is a spiritual massage session, designed to allow us to leave feeling good, tingly, happy, and relaxed. We walk out of the door having received all that God had for us, but in leaving we go out happy and content for ourselves. *WE* feel good but the *WORLD* isn't changed.

The Holy Spirit wasn't given for spiritual group-massage sessions. It was given so that we would be transformed to be transformers for the kingdom. God gives the Spirit with the intention that His immeasurably more will be transformed into immeasurably more for the world.

God gives the Spirit so that we can have a WIDER effect on His world.

FIRE EXIT

There is a sign present in all churches (it's required by law) that speaks unintentionally of a spiritual reality. Above the door (indeed possibly several doors) you will find a sign saying "FIRE EXIT", probably with a picture of a little stick man running through an open door. The fire of the Holy Spirit is needed beyond the confines of our church building or meeting space!

The Holy Spirit isn't given for the work within the church building but rather for the work of the church in the world. What happens *in here* takes place so that we might go *out there*.

The church was always called to *gather* so that we could *scatter*.

The Holy Spirit is fundamental to every Christian community and to every individual who follows Jesus.

The problem is that we as the church have bottled the Spirit and forgotten how to take the cork out.

WIDER AUTHORITY

American theologian Jonathan Edwards said, "The task of every generation is to discover the direction in which the Sovereign Redeemer is moving, and then to move in that direction."

We are a people of power and a people of authority. Jesus gave His disciples the authority to pray in His name. When we commit ourselves to Jesus with all our heart, soul, and mind, then according to Colossians 1:13 we are delivered from the "power" of darkness. This word "power" is the Greek word *exousia*, which is literally translated as "authority". When we live for Jesus we are delivered from the authority of the darkness and instead are placed under God's authority.

Jesus tells the disciples in Matthew 28:

> *All power* [exousia] *in heaven and on earth has been given to me. Therefore go and make disciples of all nations, baptizing them in the name of the Father and of the Son and of the Holy Spirit, and teaching them to obey everything I have commanded you. And surely I am with you always, to the very end of the age.*

We are delivered from one authority but given new authority.

Jesus gives His church authority to do the work set before us. We have *exousia* from heaven itself to evangelize, baptize, and teach, and to do all the works that Jesus commanded us to do.

This authority given to the disciples comes from...

OUR ADOPTION

We exercise the power given to the church because of our new family position, adoption. We are adopted into the family of God with all the rights of a child of God (John 1:12).

OUR WAITING

We exercise the power instilled during our time of waiting and surrendering to Him. In our being present to God, His presence is with us. As a result of waiting on Him we come under His authority, thus giving us authority in our turn (Acts 1:4).

OUR RELATIONSHIP

We exercise the power on the strength of our relationship with Him. In John 15 we are told that Jesus is the true vine and we are the branches; apart from Him we can do nothing (verse 5).

OUR PROPHETIC IMAGINATION

We exercise this power out of our newfound conception of what is possible. When the Holy Spirit comes, we are opened up to Him; we are closer than we imagine (Acts 1:8).

All this authority is given so that we can go more widely in the world, taking the work of the Holy Spirit to where it has not been ministered before. Jesus tells the disciples to go and make disciples of all nations. In other words, this Spirit is to go beyond our narrow human experience. This Spirit is to be offered to all people; to those we would describe as "in" and those we would describe as "out". The Spirit makes no distinction but wants to go to all people. The Spirit doesn't have the boundaries that we have.

We have a woman at church who is a devout Muslim. That's right: she's started to come to church in recent weeks, but still worships at a mosque. I asked her what made her come to church if she was a devout follower of Islam. Her answer was beautiful.

Latti said that she had woken from a dream sensing God's peace. In this dream Jesus had come to her and told her to go to church, and not just any church but *our* church. He had told her that we would tell her about Him.

It seems that Jesus is speaking in dreams and doing it without our permission. Didn't He realize she was a Muslim? Has He made a mistake? Jesus doesn't put people into the same boxes that we do, and it seems He's in the business of dismantling ours.

There are growing numbers of Muslims coming to faith – not because of courses or arguments but because God is up to something in dreams. These dreams are part of the work of the Holy Spirit. Either the Holy Spirit is making a mistake and going to the wrong people, or He is widening the remit of the religious cul-de-sac and calling more people to look to Christ than our narrow boxes allow us to think is possible. The Spirit has left the building whether we like it or not.

THE TINGLY-HAND THING

Two years ago a gang of lads in black balaclavas grabbed a man walking past our local fried chicken shop and pulled him roughly inside. The man was from E3, the postcode I live in; the lads were from E14, only half a mile down the road. They dragged him into the shop and hit and kicked him. There was blood everywhere. We called the police and they arrived fast; the man was taken away for medical checks and by God's grace he was fine.

The next day I went into the shop and spoke with the Muslim manager and two members of staff. They were incredibly shaken and wanted to close the shop early. I told them that I believed in a God of peace and provision, and that I would love to pray for them. The manager eagerly invited me to pray for him and the shop. I told them that in my tradition we held our hands out in front of us to indicate to God that we wanted to receive the gift of peace that He wanted to give to us.

In the middle of the afternoon I stood in a shop with three Muslim men with their hands held out in front of them and I prayed gently for God's holy presence to fill the shop. I said "Amen", they mumbled, and I went on my way with my tasty chicken. The reason I tell you this story is that, six months later, I was chatting to one of the members of staff when he asked me when I was going to come back and do the tingly-hand thing.

The tingly-hand thing. Amen.

In the Gospels, Jesus' desire is for all people to receive and be involved, but this confuses the disciples. On one occasion in Mark 9 the disciples find people praying for the healing of a demon-possessed man. The Holy Spirit is at work in someone who isn't a disciple, and they don't like it. John later tells Jesus how he stopped this. John doesn't like people who are not part of their group doing these things. But the Spirit doesn't have the same boundaries. John expects Jesus to be pleased and pat him on the back for preventing such a crime.

Jesus' response is simple: "Do not stop them."

The Spirit will work outside our boxes and Jesus doesn't want us to stop it, but instead to fan it!

A couple of years ago I had an email from a young guy who wanted to come and see me. We organized a time and he came round with a breathtaking story. He had been at home one night alone, drinking and doing cocaine. At about midnight he heard a voice. The voice said, "I created you to be a priest, to lead people, and you're wasting your time, money and gifts." The guy had sat talking to God for a little while and decided that he needed to see someone, so he emailed me. I asked him if he thought it was the drugs talking. (A reasonable question, I thought.) He disagreed and said this was different. It was different because he could remember every word and he had woken with a clear mind. I asked him if he knew what a priest was, and he said not really, but he knew God had clearly said he had to be one.

We prayed together and he became a Christian, and is now sorting himself out.

The Holy Spirit will do what the Holy Spirit does. We are told that if we don't praise, then the rocks will cry out, and maybe it's the same with the Spirit. What I do know to be true is that Jesus loves to work *with* us and not without us.

GREATER FOR THE WORLD

Jesus doesn't want us to be limited in any way. He doesn't want us to have small imaginations, limited by religious ways of thinking, or to be cynical, unbelieving, or unwilling. He wants to show us what it looks like to live in the power of the Spirit.

In Romans 8 we are told that the same Spirit that raised Jesus from the dead now lives in us.[1] Not a different Spirit, not a small version or a cheap taster, but the same Spirit. The word used here for "same" in the Greek literally translates as "the same". Same means same; get it?

The Spirit who was available to Jesus and whose power He showed during His ministry is available to us, right now. Sometimes we have this odd idea that Jesus was somehow different from us and that's why He could do what He did; that because He was God He had a helping hand. This is a twisted line of theology. If Jesus was somehow different from us, more spiritual, righteous, and holy, then He would have had a clear head start.

The point of the incarnation was that Jesus didn't have a head start. He was one of us, totally human. He lived differently and was more aware of what was available to Him, but He was the same. Paul makes this clear in his letter to the Philippians, saying:

Jesus who, being in very nature God, did not consider equality with God something to be used to his own advantage; rather, he made himself nothing by taking the very nature of a servant, being made in human likeness. And being found in appearance as a man, he humbled himself by becoming obedient to death – even death on a cross.[2]

Jesus humbles Himself and leaves behind equality with God so that He can identify with us. This is really important for us to grasp. If Jesus is exactly like us and yet did all those miracles, it's because He must have had something else. Yes, the Holy Spirit – and the same Spirit is now available to us. Jesus' humanity wasn't just so that His death would pay for our sin, but also to show us what we are capable of.

Jesus doesn't want us to be limited in any way, so He shows His disciples how to do the stuff and then announces to them:

> *Very truly I tell you, whoever believes in me will do the works I have been doing, and they will do even greater things than these, because I am going to the Father.*
> **John 14:12**

Jesus makes it clear that they will do the same works that He has done and then widens His encouragement: "You will do even greater things than these." Wow, greater things than Jesus – that's quite a statement. He walked on water and performed food miracles, healing miracles, resurrection miracles. How can we do greater things than the miracle of resurrection and salvation?

I don't believe that Jesus is saying greater in the sense of better, but greater in the sense of wider and more. We will see immeasurably more miracles because Jesus' work isn't over.

"Greater" is the Greek word *meizon*, meaning "to a greater degree, more". Jesus says "greater works than these", meaning a more extensive ministry.

It is also a motivating factor for us as believers while we are still living here on earth. We are to look for any opportunity, whether it be an open door to sharing, or initiating a conversation to begin to open a door. As long as there are broken lives, Jesus will be sending His Spirit to bring strength, health, love, wisdom, peace, joy, self-control, faithfulness, and unity.

GREATER WHAT?

So what is it that Jesus wants us to do more of? Paul writes to the church in Corinth to set a number of misconceptions straight.

People thought Jesus had one Spirit and we had another.

People weren't sure what the gifts were.

People thought the gifts were only for a few.

Paul writes about these gifts to clarify matters and equip the church for action.

> DIFFERENT

To the people who thought that Jesus had one Spirit and we had another, Paul wrote:

> *There are different kinds of gifts, but the same Spirit distributes them. There are different kinds of service, but the same Lord.*[3]

Different gifts, but only one Spirit: the Spirit Jesus had, the Spirit the disciples had, and the Spirit the early church experienced is the same Spirit we enjoy today.

> FEW

To the people who thought the gifts were only for a select few, Paul wrote:

> *There are different kinds of working, but in all of them and in everyone it is the same God at work.*

In the old non-politically correct version of the NIV it says, "God works all of them in all men": we would say "all people". The gifts of the Spirit are for all people. We need to grasp this and ditch the dangerous idea of the anointed few. Jesus came to show us that all people were to be called, involved, and adopted. This is why Jesus chose tax collectors and fishermen as His youth club. He showed that those poorly educated men from Galilee and the thieves who worked for Rome could all have what He had. Jesus even offered it to Nicodemus, one of the Pharisees, those hyper-religious folk.

Everyone, with no exceptions, could experience and administer the Spirit.

> MANY

When people weren't sure what the gifts were, Paul reminded them that there were many gifts to be enjoyed:

> *Now to each one the manifestation of the Spirit is given for the common good. To one there is given through the Spirit a message of wisdom, to another a message of knowledge by means of the same Spirit, to another faith by the same Spirit, to another gifts of healing by that one Spirit, to another miraculous powers, to another prophecy, to another distinguishing between spirits, to another speaking in different kinds of tongues and to still another the interpretation of tongues. All these are the work of one and the same Spirit, and he distributes them to each one, just as he determines.*[4]

Paul lists these gifts and it's like a list of the immeasurably more: wisdom, knowledge, faith, healing, miraculous powers, prophecy, discernment, tongues, and the interpretation of tongues. Later in the letter, in chapter 12, verse 28, he lists the assets that God has placed in the church. He names them as apostles, prophets, teachers, miracle workers, those with gifts of healing, helpers, administrators, and again those who speak God's heavenly language.

Paul's list is meant to increase our idea of what the gifts are and encourage us to want more of them. The one spiritual gift that many overlook and don't view as important is that of administration. Without the work of the administrators, those who serve in other ways wouldn't be enabled. It's the work of those who administrate that keeps things on track, keeps things going, and keeps things organized for God's glory.

EAGERLY DESIRE

We need to want the gifts of the Spirit; our self-sufficiency and belief in our ability to cope reflects our strength and resilience as human beings but also reveals how pathetically proud we are. If we showed that we needed all the gifts God offers to us, it would prove that we're not as strong as we think and that God is greater than we think.

It's our pride that is our downfall. We're weary and worn out, feeling fragile and under-equipped. You just have to look at people's faces on a Monday morning. A weekend of rest isn't enough; we're scraping along at rock bottom and just about making it through. Our pride stops us from desiring the help we so desperately need and also from getting on our knees and asking for it.

> *We are in fact very like honest but reluctant taxpayers. We approve of an income tax in principle. We make our returns truthfully. But we dread a rise in the tax. We are very careful to pay no more than is necessary. And we hope – we very ardently hope – that after we have paid it there will still be enough left to live on.*[5]
> C. S. Lewis

Like the taxpayer, we don't want to pay more than we have to, and in the same way we don't want to give away more to God than we have to. But this isn't about giving more away; it's about creating room to *receive* more. Paul writes to the people of Corinth that they should "eagerly desire the greater gifts"[6] and then later "desire the special abilities the Spirit gives".[7]

Paul wants us to crave these gifts but we behave as if they are a spiritual extra, to be sought if we fancy it or if we really have to (i.e. reluctantly). Paul uses the Greek word *zeloo*, which we translate as "eagerly" but which can also mean "to set one's heart on something that belongs to someone else" – "to covet". It is, of course, also possible to interpret it as meaning "to be envious" or "to be jealous".

Paul tells us to *eagerly desire* these gifts, to be green-eyed; to crave them, covet them, long for them, enthusiastically stretching out our arms and impatiently, zealously, fervently wanting them. Not a pathetic, half-hearted wish, but a deep longing for immeasurably more of God's Spirit.

PRAYER

Father, we come to You, praying in the name and by the authority of Your Son, Jesus.

We pray for Your widening work of the Spirit in us, that we would have a greater imagination, a greater sense of Your power, and a greater passion for transformed lives.

Our prayer is that You would use us to see the works of Your kingdom transform the lives of those we live with, those we work with, and those we see only on TV screens and in photos. We pray that You will use us in ways we never dreamed were possible, for Your glory.

Amen.

Immeasurably More: Small-Group Study

QUESTION: Jesus was able to perform amazing miraculous signs. Do you think He was able to do these because He was God, or because He had the Holy Spirit?

QUESTION: Do you think there is any hope of our doing miracles if we aren't God?

We are about to find out in the reading that we have within us the same Spirit that raised Jesus from the dead. Jesus by becoming human had given up special powers. Jesus works wonders as someone who is showing us that a perfect relationship with God means an empowered life. Jesus' miracles aren't done because He is God but because He has the Holy Spirit within Him.

At this point, pray that as we read the passage the Holy Spirit would reveal to us what He is wanting to say through it.

READ: Romans 8:9–17

What jumps out from this passage?

Do you notice something you haven't seen before or don't understand?

What is God saying to you in this reading?

QUESTION: In verse 11, it says: "If the Spirit of him who raised Jesus from the dead is living in you, he who raised Christ from the dead will also give life to your mortal bodies." What's your reaction to knowing that the Spirit of Resurrection Sunday is at work in you? Are you overwhelmed? Excited? Worried?

QUESTION: Children carry the family likeness. Verse 14 says that If we are led by the Spirit, we are children of God. What is the family likeness that we now share?

QUESTION: The Holy Spirit gives life, and this life now lives in us. Miracles are moments when life is given back to something or someone. A broken limb is given new life in a healing. Have you ever experienced this kind of new life?

QUESTION: Someone coming to know God as Abba, Father, is a miracle in itself. Have you ever thought about salvation being a miracle?

QUESTION: What is the glory that we now share in, which is talked about in verse 17?

PRAY

Spend some time praying that this Spirit within you will help you to live out this engaging faith you have in Jesus. Also pray that this faith wouldn't be simply a head faith but also a faith lived out in prayer and petition for the further work of the Spirit in the world around you. Ask God to give you opportunities to pray for miracles and the confidence to keep praying if you don't see something straight away.

WHAT GOT YOU HERE WILL NOT
GET YOU THERE.
Marshall Goldsmith

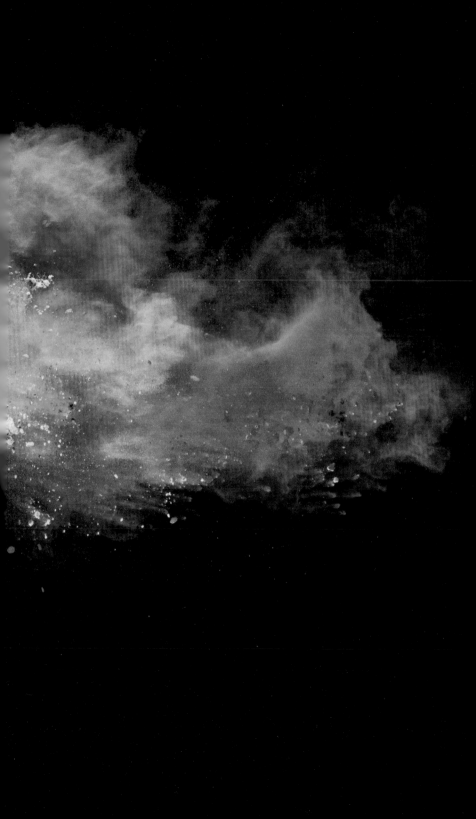

A Further Story
A real story about people called Rachel and Alan

Alan and I married in 1982 and went on to live in a lovely detached home with friendly neighbours, within walking distance of town. We had a good church with great worship, and good friends and relationships. All in all, life in Basingstoke was very comfortable.

As retirement approached we realized that, although for some people this time is about winding down, God still had work for us to do.

In the last few years we sensed the Spirit prompting and stirring us to get involved with new opportunities to serve people and love them for Jesus. Then in 2010 my mum died, which left us feeling that we could be released from Basingstoke, and with our youngest graduating in 2011 and getting married in 2012, we no longer needed a large home.

While attending a conference that year we were alerted by the Holy Spirit to the huge challenge posed by Britain's urban and multicultural areas. We felt that Jesus had come to the least advantaged, and wanted to look at how we might do the same and stop living in comfy, leafy suburbia! So we started to explore joining a church in a rough urban area. A friend of ours at this point mentioned the Eden Network to us, and it's been Eden that's helped us relocate to one of the toughest communities in the country to live out Jesus' incarnation, pitching in and becoming local to see lives transformed. The vision excited us and the Spirit inspired us to answer this call, so with Eden we have ventured out to take the gospel into places and to a generation that have never heard it in their language.

This call to us meant a move to a more challenging area. No way could we have gone back to the beautiful place where we were living for so many years. **The Holy Spirit had made us feel uncomfortable and challenged us to get up and move with Him.** Having found a church with a local vision, with a desire to make Jesus known in its needy community, we both knew it was the right place for us. We believe we have found like-minded people in this church, although we all need to constantly encourage one another and challenge each other in our following of God. We love the grace that abounds and are delighted to be stretched in this too!

It's the Holy Spirit that's become the renewing and refreshing power in me, although it is also the uncomfortable Spirit that pushes us to go further with Him into the lives of those that just don't get it. It's a push that makes us go further than we have gone before, and long to hand on this faith to the next generation for the future.

MOVEMENT
FIVE
FURTHER

FOR EVER AND EVER! AMEN.
Ephesians 3:21b

As we arrive at this final movement, we are going to look at how the Spirit empowers God's people to go "further" into the future and into the lives of people needing His grace. We are going to look first at the problem of crippling disbelief in God and see that there is hope. Second, we will look at the disciples and at how the Spirit caused the gospel to spiral out from Jerusalem to the ends of the earth: this gospel was always meant to go somewhere. We will end by considering the purpose of all this: seeing God meeting the needs of people and transforming lives — not in church services but in the unique and momentary interactions of life.

1 FORWARD THROUGH DISBELIEF

We have this idea that there was a time in Christian history that we call the "early church", which we look back at and learn from and hope to imitate. But, as Dr Rowan Williams once pointed out, "for all we know we are still the early church". God's plan is that the church will continue into the future for as long as it is needed as we wait for Jesus' return. We might still be the early church. Ponder that for a moment.

Imagine future generations looking at us and speaking of us as those early Christians. Maybe the church of the future will look at this moment in church history as the time when the church took courageous steps forward in what it was, and became more empowered to do the stuff.

Jesus' plan was that His church would be Plan A until the day He returned. The church is His only plan; He has no other alternative up His sleeve. This means that Jesus intends it to keep going into the future, like a lonely cowboy plodding off into the sunset at the end of a western. The adventure goes on; it didn't start with us and it will probably not end with us.

Jesus had died and the disciples had done a runner; they had gone back to their old lives with the belief that there was no future. It was all over; they had put all their eggs in one basket and that basket was now empty. But the God of the Jewish people wasn't a God of endings; He's the God of new beginnings. This meant the plan was not over; in fact, it was only just beginning. The tomb cracks open and Jesus, filled with the Spirit, is resurrected from the dead. A new day is born and the future suddenly opens up with endless possibilities. Those who are trapped now have the hope of freedom; those who are lost can be found, and those who are broken can be made whole. Jesus is back and there is no longer any fear of death but a new fear: the fear of eternity. What will that look like? I don't know about you, but to me eternity sounds exciting but also scary.

The resurrection and then the outpouring of the Holy Spirit cracks open a new future that has immeasurably more about it. The future is no longer stark, but buzzing with expectation. Jesus commissions the disciples, and churches are built – not of bricks and mortar but around people and an idea of resurrection life. Death has now lost its sting for this church, and its excited people are filled with fresh anticipation.

Wow! Doesn't this sound wonderful: new hope, new dreams, and new possibilities? Everything is glorious and everything is perfect. Don't we want to be a part of a church like that?

BUT...

But, indeed. Although miracles are seen and the church grows, people are still involved and arguments occur; miracles don't always end as people expect, and the questions start to arise.

"When is Jesus coming back?"

The early church had a belief that Jesus' return was imminent and that one day, maybe in a few weeks (but hopefully not years), He would reappear. The result of this was a desire to live "full-on" for Jesus because He would be coming back soon.

"Jesus is coming! Look busy."

But the weeks roll on, wonders and miraculous things happen, though maybe not as often as they had hoped, and people's spirits begin to droop. Paul writes to the churches exhorting them to keep going, as Jesus *will* return, but even he initially thought it would be sooner than it was.

The church grows and lives are changed, miracles continue but less often, people prophesy and dream dreams, the Spirit is at work. At some points it looks as if things are going well in the church and at other times things dip. There are ages when the church is lost and ages when the church is blooming. The adventure goes on further into the future. Wars happen and people find hope in this resurrection that once occurred. Science and modern thinking challenge people about the authenticity of these old stories of gods, miracles, and resurrections. We start to question whether it even happened. Were people mistaken; did it really happen? We start to question Jesus, who He was, and whether He had children and a wife. The church becomes disillusioned, confused, and lost, falling back into "religion".

But there is hope because we believe in the God of resurrection: from death to life. And each time it looks as if the church is about to die the Spirit breathes new life into it. Prophets speak and call it back to the original manifesto to practise resurrection and wait on the Spirit. To look HIGHER, draw CLOSER, go DEEPER, open up WIDER, and go FURTHER.

FORWARD BUT NOT YET

As we head into the future we have the hope of endless possibilities, but the heartbreak of unanswered prayer, miracles never seen, and hopes dashed can leave a church feeling jaded and defeatist. The church lives in this moment of now and not yet. It's an awkward time, during which we hope and dream but don't always see.

It's like a package ordered online: you know it's coming but you can't guarantee when it will arrive, and if you're anything like me (with our post occasionally getting lost) it sometimes seems that it's not coming at all.

The kingdom is on order but it has not yet arrived. It's the kingdom pending, dispatched, or in transit.

HOLY SATURDAY – GOD IS DEAD

We walk into the future with a sense of anticipation vying with a deep sense of grief. These feelings of hope and grief are rooted in the heart of the Easter story. They stem from a day about which little is preached, and which is largely glossed over by the evangelical church. We gather together on Good Friday, we deal with our grief at the loss of Christ, and then we arrive on the Sunday to celebrate the resurrection. But there is a day in between that tends to be skipped but which holds within it the raw pain of aching uncertainty.

Little is said about Holy Saturday in the Gospels. This day rests between death and life and leaves the world with more questions than answers. Holy Saturday is a day of silence, confusion, and bewilderment.

It's a day marked in traditional churches by stripping the altars bare. The grief is reflected in the lack of colour and decoration.

In some Eastern Orthodox churches they have a short gathering where little or nothing is said. It's a day when we don't have answers: we have little to say; nothing to add. All the candles and lights in the church are extinguished, and everyone waits in darkness and silence for the proclamation of the resurrection of Christ.

> *Holy Saturday seems to me to describe the place in which many of us live our lives: waiting for God to speak. We know that Jesus died for us yesterday. We trust that there may be miracles tomorrow. But what of today – this eternal Sabbath when heaven is silent? Where, we wonder, is God now?*[1]
> **Pete Greig**

In stillness the earth awaits the resurrection.

We live in this place.

What is happening? Today there is a great silence over the earth, a great silence, and stillness, a great silence because the King sleeps; the earth was in terror and was still, because God slept in the flesh and raised up those who were sleeping from the ages. God has died in the flesh, and the underworld has trembled.[2]

To be a church that runs into the future with excitement about what *could* and *will* happen, we also need to be a church that grieves for the pain and agony of a world that is not yet. Not because God isn't capable – He can certainly do immeasurably more – but because He's wanting to work through it with us. Jesus is the God of partnership.

God's kingdom is both *now* and *not yet*. It is present in certain respects, and future in others. Our Lord came proclaiming and demonstrating that the kingdom which is the rule and reign of God had intersected with human history.

NEAR? AT HAND? HERE? THERE? IN OUR MIDST?

In Matthew 3:2 Jesus announces that the *"kingdom of heaven has come near"*, and in Mark 1:15 that *"the kingdom of God is at hand".* Then in the Gospel of Luke, chapter 17, verse 21, Jesus says that people will not say *"'Here it is,' or 'There it is,' because the kingdom of God is in your midst"*.

So where is it: near, at hand, here, there, or in our midst? The truth is that the answer to all of them is yes. The kingdom is neither near, at hand, here, there, or in our midst but at the same time it *is* near, at hand, here, there, and in our midst. The answer is yes.

Well, isn't that confusing!

God's kingdom has come and it is here, but at the same time it has not yet come in its fullness and it won't do so until Jesus returns in power, when every knee will bow and every tongue will confess that He is Lord. Until then, without denying the present reality of God's kingdom, we fervently pray, "May Your kingdom come."

In the heavenly realms everything has changed. We are adopted, the debts are settled, and in the high court of heaven we are chosen, freed, healed, redeemed, restored, and reinstated. But on this side of heaven our internal transformation is an ongoing project.

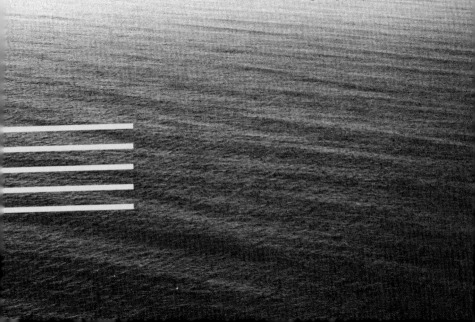

VE DAY VS D-DAY

There are many ways of viewing this "now but not yet". There is no better illustration than that of World War Two. Oscar Cullmann offers this compelling image:

> *The decisive battle in a war may already have occurred in a relatively early stage of the war, and yet the war still continues. Although the decisive effect of that battle is perhaps not recognized by all, it nevertheless already means victory. But the war must still be carried on for an undefined time, until Victory Day.*[3]

Cullmann is alluding to D-Day and VE Day. During the Second World War D-Day occurred on 6 June 1944 when there was an extensive battle in which the Allies were victorious. The Allied forces landed on the beaches of Normandy and began to invade and reclaim France from the Germans. This is now seen as a turning point and a key element in winning the whole war. Once the troops had successfully landed and completed that battle, Hitler's fate was sealed. The war was essentially over. However, the actual war in Europe was not finally won until VE (Victory in Europe) Day on 7 May 1945, when the German forces surrendered in Berlin.

Although the enemy had been mortally wounded at D-Day, he did not immediately succumb.

Good Friday is our D-Day. The day that Jesus died was the day that the war was won, we were set free, and His work was finished. Yet there is still a final victory to be won on Christ's return. As with D-Day, there is no doubt as to the outcome of the war, but we will still find ourselves involved in the ongoing spiritual battle until the spiritual equivalent of VE Day when Jesus returns in glory to vanquish the forces of darkness for ever.

We now live in between D-Day and VE Day.

IMMEASURABLY MORE IN THE IN BETWEEN

We might therefore think that all we are facing are years of difficulty and pain, but this simply isn't true. We believe in the God of immeasurably more. Yes, we continue to hope and dream, expanding our imagination to encompass what is possible, but on the other hand we also have a God who gives more in the pain and in the disappointments.

Just because something hasn't gone the way we planned, it doesn't mean that God is powerless. In fact, He never promised us an easy ride, but He does promise us a safe arrival.

What the cross reminds us is that God has...

Immeasurably more in our grief.

Immeasurably more in our pain.

Immeasurably more in our disappointments.

Immeasurably more in our suffering.

Jesus never claimed that we would avoid hard times and struggles, but He assures us that we can know the closeness of the God of more in the midst of them. Jesus promises us restoration in our grief, restoration in our pain, restoration in our disappointment, and restoration in our suffering.

The God of more promises His presence in the midst of the suffering; He promises His goodness, love, mercy, joy, peace, and provision.

The God of more is the God of more in the presence of pain and in the absence of it. He's the God of more in the miracle of healing and in the sadness of death. The God of more is the same God who breathes life into a newborn and receives the life of an elderly person. In the dark times and in the light, God is the God of *immeasurably more*.

What does this mean for us as we move forward? It means that whatever happens, we can be sure that Jesus is with us. When we pray and nothing happens, Jesus is with us because our VE Day is coming. When we lose a loved one, VE Day is coming. When a newborn is lost moments after birth, VE Day is coming.

And in this moment of waiting between the death and the resurrection, the "God who comforts the downcast, comforted us".[4]

God has immeasurably more for us in our grief because He comforts us. When life falls on us like an overwhelming torrent of water, we are told: "When you pass through the waters, God will be with you; and through the rivers, they shall not overwhelm you; when you walk through fire you shall not be burned, and the flame shall not consume you."[5]

God has so much more to give in protecting us. As David puts it, "He who dwells in the shelter of the Most High will abide in the shadow of the Almighty. I will say to the Lord, 'My refuge and my fortress, my God, in whom I trust.'"[6]

FOCUSING ON WHAT GOD HAS DONE

What we mustn't do is see unanswered prayer as the absence of God; rather, it is an opportunity for God to reveal more of His presence. When we are in that Holy Saturday place, the presence of God is there to reveal more of His love. It's in this place that we need to focus on what God has already done, and not on what He hasn't yet done. There are many things that God hasn't done, but far more that He has.

One moment of drinking from the cup of *hasn't done* will dishearten us and leave us discouraged. In the same way, one sip from the cup of *has done* will encourage us, give us hope, and spur us on to keep praying for more.

Immeasurably More: Small-Group Study

QUESTION: God promises us that He will be with us for ever and ever. But sometimes it doesn't feel like it. What things have left you feeling that God is absent or not listening?

QUESTION: Do you have any answers for where God is in the absence?

QUESTION: If a non-believer asked you where God was in the suffering of a family who had just lost a child, or in a major community disaster, what would you say? How would you speak about God?

At this point, pray that as we read the passage the Holy Spirit would reveal to us what He is wanting to say through it.

READ: Psalm 91

What jumps out from this passage?

Do you notice something you haven't seen before or don't understand?

What is God saying to you in this reading?

QUESTION: In the passage, statements are made about God's presence with people. It speaks of people dwelling in God's shelter or resting in God's shadow. Have you ever experienced this as a reality? How?

QUESTION: When has this sheltering in God not felt real or tangible for you?

QUESTION: In verse 10 it says that if we commit ourselves to the Lord no disaster will come upon us. Yet if we look at history, many devout Christians have been struck by ill health, disaster, and untimely death. Is the passage strictly true or is it trying to say something deeper?

QUESTION: How do we juggle God's promise of His presence and the feeling of His absence?

Is there a danger of focusing on what we feel over what we know to be true?

When you pass through the waters, God will be with you; and through the rivers, they shall not overwhelm you; when you walk through fire you shall not be burned, and the flame shall not consume you.
Isaiah 43:2

QUESTION: There is this tension that we experience as Christians between the moment when the battle over evil was won on the cross and the time of God's full reign upon Jesus' return. We wait in a place of promise, with glimmers of light in the darkness. What do you think we as Christians need to hold on to as we go into an uncertain future?

QUESTION: What are you dealing with at the moment from which you need to experience God's shelter? Are you able to pray that God would do something amazing in this area of your life?

PRAY

Jesus promises us that He will be with us to the very end of the age. His promise is that, even though we await His return and the final moment of completion of His plans, He will remain with us. Spend some time praying that this would become a reality for you and that His presence would hold you in times when life feels unstable.

2 FURTHER INTO THE WORLD

As a church that is honest about grief, we also need to be empowered for hope. And not just hope, but a power that will lead us to be the church that Jesus intended. The book of Acts starts with Jesus standing with His disciples. Jesus is just about to ascend into heaven and the disciples are standing before Him. Jesus makes them a promise, which was for them but also for the world:

> You will receive power when the Holy Spirit comes on you, and you will be my witnesses in Jerusalem, and in all Judea and Samaria, and to the ends of the earth.[1]

There are a few things we need to note here. The disciples up to this point had been pretty pathetic. They were slow to understand, unclear in their speaking, and not always sure what they were doing. Jesus tells them that when the Holy Spirit comes upon them they will receive power. The Greek word used here is *dunamis*; it is often translated as "power" or "authority" but is actually where we get the word "dynamite". When we receive the Holy Spirit it's as if we will have dynamite. Dynamite in our prayers, dynamite to get things done, and dynamite in our words. The disciples prove this to be true. They go from ill-educated fishermen to becoming the most powerful preachers and teachers of the gospel since Jesus Himself. The Holy Spirit unlocks something within the disciples. They become like dynamite.

But why do they need to be like dynamite? This outpouring is about the disciples having what they need to thrive; receiving all that God has for them. And the consequence of this is that everything is different: their confidence and who they believe themselves to be. They see the truth of their sin and the good news of the cross.

Everything starts to make sense.

This outpouring of the Spirit has a purpose.

SPIRALS

Jesus says that when they have received this Spirit they will become witnesses *in Jerusalem, and in all Judea and Samaria, and to the ends of the earth*. The choice of places is significant. It's about more than just being witnesses all over the world. Each of these locations represents a particular place or group that really needs to hear the gospel. It's a list that spirals out from the epicentre to the edges.

JERUSALEM

First, Jerusalem. Jesus makes it clear that they are to witness to the religious epicentre. It was here that the Spirit was first poured out. There is a strong argument that the Holy Spirit didn't come in an upper room in a house but in the Temple itself. The term used for "house" in the passage could be translated as "the house of God", the Temple. This could explain why they so quickly find themselves in the Temple preaching. Nevertheless, they are to witness to the religious world in the city. "Jerusalem" today would be our church communities who are sure of their religious faith.

JUDEA

Judea was less "religious" but still committed to faith in the God of Abraham. Rather than being the hard-headed religionists, these were the curious people who wanted to experience more than what Jerusalem could offer. If Jerusalem represents the religious city, then Judea represents the religious countryside. Judea stands for those who believed but were somehow outside the faith epicentre. We might say people of faith who were seeking more than what had previously been on offer.

SAMARIA

Going a little further out, we now hit a mountainous region called Samaria. This is where the unclean Samaritans lived. The Jewish people had a deep-seated racist hatred of the Samaritans and detested their presence. There was a long-standing feud between them that had become an issue argued hotly by both sides. The Samaritans were seen as unholy, unclean, and unworthy, but Jesus says that the Spirit will lead the disciples to witness to this unclean religious bunch.

A Jewish book called *Mishna Sheviit* (section 8:10) reads: "He that eats the bread of the Samaritans is like to one who eats the flesh of pigs." The Jews saw pigs as an unclean, almost demonic animal that you would not dare to go near or touch. The Jewish writer Ben Sirach, who lived 200 years before Jesus, wrote: "There are two nations I detest. The third is not a nation at all, the inhabitants of Mount Seir and the Philistines and the stupid people of Shechem." These stupid people at Shechem were the Samaritans.

The picture had thus been painted that the Samaritans were so absorbed in a misplaced idea of God that the Jewish people had been dehumanizing them. The Samaritans represent those of other faiths that had been devalued and almost demonized.

THE ENDS OF THE EARTH

Jesus then sends the disciples out to the edges of the world. If Jerusalem represents the religious, then the ends of the earth represent the irreligious. This is the pagan world, which is non-religious or worships distinctly *evil* gods. The Jewish people had tended to stick within their own community. Only through displacement had they found themselves away from the religious community of Jerusalem, Judea, and the surrounding land.

In the story of the prodigal son we are told that he has gone to a distant land where pigs are being kept. The symbol here is of a land where pigs are elevated while farmhands starve. The world "out there" had been seen as lost, pagan, and dark. Jesus tells His disciples that because of the Holy Spirit's witnessing to the ends of the earth, even these pagan worlds are saveable.

If the witnessing of the disciples has to start with the religious world, then it's going to end with the non-religious world.

Imagine how strange and scary that would have sounded to them, but that's what happens with the God of immeasurably more. The Holy Spirit always leads us into a further engagement with evangelism.

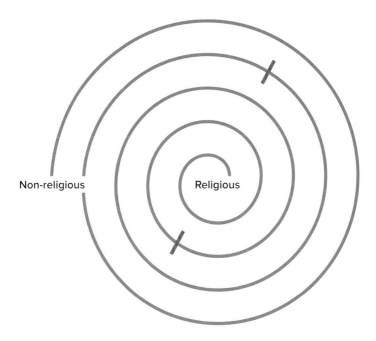

Activity

Starting at the centre of the spiral, name the Christian world you live in. As you journey out from the centre, mark the growing number of non-religious places you travel to. For the last third of the spiral, think about the places you would fear going to – the ones that you would struggle to make the trip to because of the degree to which it would take you out of your comfort zone.

QUESTION: Who and what are the people, places, and streets that you would struggle to go to?

QUESTION: Who is your "Samaria and ends of the earth"?

FURTHER OUT

The work of the Holy Spirit pushes the church further out than it has been before, and the same is true with us. When the work of the Holy Spirit is truly transforming us, then it will bubble over into our naturally sharing our lives with people and pointing them to Jesus.

The best thing we can offer a broken and hurting world is the life and goodness of the Lord. And the way we do that is to spend time with Him, soaking in His presence. So that who He is rubs off on us. So that we go out not as insurance salesmen selling a product, but as people who live in His presence, dwell in His presence, and move in His presence. It's from that place that everything changes.

We struggle with evangelism. The very word makes some people's skin crawl and others have that sick feeling when it's mentioned. Evangelism is hard, embarrassing, and often fruitless. But what the disciples found on the day of Pentecost was that this pointing people to Jesus became second nature; the embarrassment was worth it and it became incredibly fruitful.

THE SPIRIT IS ON ME...

Three years earlier Jesus had been at the synagogue in Nazareth, and on being handed the scroll of Isaiah He read from chapter 61. Many have argued that this was similar to the start of a political campaign. Jesus is setting out His manifesto. "If you want to know what My mission statement is, then here goes..."

Jesus reads:

> *The Spirit of the Lord is on me,*
> *because he has anointed me*
> *to proclaim good news to the poor.*
> *He has sent me to proclaim freedom for*
>   *the prisoners*
> *and recovery of sight for the blind,*
> *to set the oppressed free,*
> *to proclaim the year of the Lord's favour.*

The Spirit of the Lord is on me *because*...

The word "because" is probably one of the most essential words in this passage, and often gets overlooked: the Spirit for Isaiah and now for Jesus was poured out for a purpose. We don't receive the Spirit simply to allow us to enjoy God's presence but so that we will *do* something with it.

The Spirit is poured out *because* God wants to anoint us *for* something. The Spirit comes to anoint us. Anointing is about a sacramental or divine influence over a person or thing; it's a holy emanation or holy emission. Something that is anointed has had the presence of God placed upon it, and in it. The Spirit is there to anoint us and set us apart, giving us power so that we will have everything we need for the furthering of the kingdom.

Jesus says He has been anointed for: witnessing to the good news, announcing freedom for prisoners, healing the blind, unburdening the oppressed, and proclaiming that God's plan is to free people from the debt of sin.

So the Spirit is poured out *FOR* something.

Jesus has the Spirit to bring justice, bring healing, bless the poor, and restore the broken.

Jesus makes no mention of the Spirit being poured out for worship times, ministry times, or church services. It's not that the Spirit doesn't want to be involved in those things, but that for Jesus the "because" is for bigger, further, and wider things. Jesus has the Spirit not for Himself but for others, and the same is true of us. This same Spirit now anoints us "because" we are to be set apart for bringing justice, bringing healing, blessing the poor, and restoring the broken.

The Spirit is poured out so that we would hear the good news and share it.

The Spirit is poured out so that we would be freed from sin and be able to free others from prisons.

The Spirit is poured out for our healing and to enable the healing of others through us.

The Spirit is poured out so that we would be released and so that we would release others who are battered and bruised.

The Spirit is poured out so that we would receive freedom from debt and so that we would free others.

QUESTION: What does Jesus' mission look like here?

QUESTION: How do we know what Jesus' mission is?

HEAVEN COME TO EARTH

The work of the Holy Spirit has been misunderstood for so long. We think it behaves like a prop to hold us up, but it's much more than this. The Spirit comes because He wants us to partner with Him. God hates working alone; He loves people, and wants to work with us.

> *The key message of Easter is not "Jesus is alive again, and therefore we're all going to heaven".*
>
> *If you look at the gospel resurrection narratives in Matthew, Mark, Luke and John and the beginning of Acts, none of them say "Jesus is alive again, and therefore we're all going to heaven". Later on in the New Testament, it says it again and again: Our future is bound up with what happened – the point about the resurrection is that "Jesus has been raised from the dead, and therefore God's New Creation has begun, and therefore we have a job to do."*
>
> *And I suspect some of the insistence on instantly talking about "going to heaven" in the Western church may have been a displacement activity – because the job we have been given in creation is so demanding and challenging. It's much easier to think "Ah – end of story – now it's all right and we don't need to worry any more".*
>
> *Well, you don't need to worry any more, but you do need to work.*[2]

The gospel isn't about a mass evacuation to paradise, but about the renewal of all things. Therefore, the work of the Spirit is about equipping us with the tools we need to see heaven come to earth.

God plans immeasurably more for His church than just gathering, singing, preaching, and praying. He offers a life that is empowered by the Spirit so that we can be involved in the miraculous. Jesus wants a radically empowered church to seek healing, seek freedom, and seek justice. Justice for the kingdom is just as miraculous as seeing eyes opened from blindness.

We sometimes have this idea that there are "real" works of the kingdom and then there are earthly works of the kingdom. Let me explain. A debt management programme that is led by the Spirit is just as much a work of the kingdom as someone being healed from cancer. A young person being mentored and directed away from crime is as much a work of the kingdom as a healing miracle.

The physical world is directly tied up with the spiritual world. That's why when we have delivered a chest of drawers or a TV to someone in need on our estate we have often had the joy of praying for a miracle with them. People's lives aren't as compartmentalized into "sacred" and "secular" as we might think. If we are meeting someone's physical needs because of the work of the Spirit in us, then it's as much a miracle as meeting a spiritual need.

A knee being healed is physical: it's limbs and ligaments and bones; the Spirit is over all creation from dust, hovering over water and seeing blood, sweat, and tears being used to build an expansive new kingdom. It's both physical and spiritual at the same time.

The Spirit of the Lord is upon us because He wants us to pray for the healing of the sick *and* proclaim freedom from credit card debt. The Spirit of the Lord is upon us because He wants us to lead people to a living relationship with Jesus *and* see justice done for a widow.

Being anointed by the Spirit means that we are becoming more naturally supernatural. As we become more involved in the Spirit's work we realize that the purpose of this Spirit isn't to "get more of it" (the Spirit) but to enable us to give more of ourselves away. The Spirit leads us to a place where we can create more space for Him in our lives. This in turn allows more scope for us to give to Him and to others.

SO WHAT DOES THE SPIRIT DO?

The Spirit of God anoints us to do quite a few things...

- He draws us further into His presence, like waves on a beach.

- He strengthens us for what lies ahead.

- He brings clarity and inspiration to our lives and the world around us.

- He changes us more into His likeness.

- He gives us power to see miracles.

- He encourages us to be devoted to mission.

The Spirit propels us further into the world, just as the disciples were sent out into all the world. The Spirit comes to encourage us and equip us for action. He comes that we might move, work, and act.

The Holy Spirit comes so that our workplaces, homes, streets, neighbourhoods, nurseries, youth clubs, buses, and supermarkets might become humming with the possibility of people finding Him. The Holy Spirit comes so that, wherever we find ourselves, we might have the opportunity to point people to Jesus. Sadly, our mission has become one of convincing people that our product is better than the other products on the shelves. We argue, we twist arms, and we coerce people. We even try to trick them by asking them to come to "Pie and Mash nights" as normal social events and then subjecting them to some evangelistic message for the price of a free meal. Evangelism in the pages of the New Testament is a collision of truth and fire.

TRUTH AND FIRE

The advance of the early church did not come about merely through the preaching of the good news but also through the evidence of the power of God in their midst. Time after time, it's the message of forgiveness and then the demonstration of power that leads people to see the breadth of God.

The message of the gospel is truth accompanied by experienced reality... God verified its truthfulness by a display of his own power through the ministry of the Holy Spirit.[3]

Look at the story of Moses. As he led the people out of Egypt, it was the power of the demonstration of signs and wonders, such as the opening of the Red Sea, that showed that the message he was preaching was also a message of truth, built on the reality of a living God.

The story of Gideon is a story of truth being proclaimed, but when he beat the Midianites with only 300 men it was God's power that made the people victorious, not their clever tactics.

The truth of Jesus has to be preached; it's central to people hearing the message. The fire of the Holy Spirit also needs to be experienced for someone to learn the truth of it. We need to remember that the presence of God's Spirit and the miracles that follow aren't simply signs of the kingdom of God, but an essential part of it.

It has been my experience that other cultures don't have a problem with holding the truth and the fire together. My experience has been that they accept it as though it's true. **If a God of resurrection lives, then why wouldn't miracles follow?** Look at the church in China, Africa, and Asia: its growth there is characterized by such signs and wonders of the kingdom.

The Holy Spirit was designed to be present in God's people and to work in and through them so that they should become to the world the very thing that the Spirit first brought to them... Good News.

As Paul writes to the Corinthians, "My message and my preaching were not with wise and persuasive words, but with *a demonstration of the Spirit's power*, so that your faith might not rest on human wisdom, but on God's power."[4]

The Spirit comes to demonstrate what is true, so that our message will have weight, validity, and evidence. Paul realized that his words could have been taken as merely human wisdom, but it was the work of the Spirit that proved they were true. It's the demonstration of the Spirit's power that waters the seeds planted by the message we have sown.

Immeasurably More: Small-Group Study

QUESTION: God has a plan for His church, and it's not waiting for some mass evacuation to heaven. We misunderstand the gospel if we think it's simply about getting to heaven. God wants His church to be involved here on earth. What do you think He wants it to be involved in?

QUESTION: Why do you think we are given the Holy Spirit? What's His purpose?

At this point, pray that as we read the passage the Holy Spirit would reveal to us what He is wanting to say through it.

READ: Luke 4:18–19

What jumps out from this passage?

Do you notice something you haven't seen before or don't understand?

What is God saying to you in this reading?

QUESTION: For what purposes does the passage say the Holy Spirit is given?

QUESTION: God intends immeasurably more for His church than just gathering, singing, preaching, and praying. If a church gathering is about His people being anointed, what should a regular week for a Christian look like? What *should* we be doing?

QUESTION: How much of our time is actually spent on the things mentioned in the passage?

QUESTION: How does the passage play out in reality in your area? In what ways are the broken-hearted being bound up and the captives set free?

QUESTION: The Spirit is given to propel us further into a broken world. What do you think the Spirit might be guiding you into?

QUESTION: If Jesus wants His church to go further in the future, what new things do you think the Spirit might be leading the church into? We often like to stay in our comfort zones, but the Spirit leads us out of comfort into the grit of real life. Where might this be? What might this look like?

QUESTION: In the passage, the outworking of the Spirit is both practical (binding up) and spiritual (the forgiveness of sins). Which do you think the church is better at dealing with?

PRAY

Lord, would You send Your Spirit on us that we might be anointed to proclaim good news to the poor? Please anoint us to proclaim freedom for the prisoners, to see healing miracles for the blind, to set the oppressed free, and to announce Your forgiveness and favour over people. Amen.

Spend some time praying that the group would receive a fresh anointing of the Spirit so that they might live according to the gospel in their community. Pray that the Lord might lead the group to a new place of living out the gospel, empowered by His Holy Spirit.

---

3 MORE IN THE NORMAL AND THE MUNDANE

ALL THE NATIONS MAY WALK IN
THE NAME OF THEIR GODS, BUT WE
WILL WALK IN THE NAME OF THE
LORD OUR GOD FOR EVER AND
EVER.

Micah 4:5

We are tired, aren't we? But this isn't the end: Jesus has more for us to do, further for us to run, and more Spirit for us to experience. That might fill some of us with the dread of "I just can't keep going; I'm finished". You're not alone in that thought, and thank you for your honesty.

God looks at us and wants us to "go" further with Him.

The relationship is only just starting; we have eternity ahead of us and God wants us to go much further with Him. It's as if He can see what's laid out before us and He's excited by what it means for us. Each thing that is set before us is a challenge and an experiment, but it certainly all ends up as an adventure.

God has more for our relationship than what we have yet experienced. In any good marriage the couple grow closer together, get to know each other better, and work better in partnership. As the years roll on, the closeness gets deeper. They may say that they love each other more now than on the day they married. It's as if the years have refined the relationship and both are more comfortable with each other than before. They end each other's sentences, know instinctively when something is up, and communicate telepathically. Well, maybe not that last one – or perhaps my wife and I just aren't there yet...

God wants to go further with us in the years ahead: to grow closer, for us to know each other better, and (from God's side) to give us more of what we need to thrive.

It can seem, as we go about our daily business with God, that there isn't much to celebrate. We get up, have a wash, have some breakfast, drink a cup of coffee, check for nose hair, and walk out of the door ready for a new day at work. It can seem monotonous – "same old same old" – and completely empty of inspiration, and we wonder how this day can be used for anything other than the bland.

Life is normal; life is what it is: it rolls on and on and we can't always see how what we hope for in God and what happens in our life hang together. So how do we carry on like this and see it any differently?

The question is: How do we have an authentic, Jesus-centred life, a real relationship with Him, while running the race in a phony, superficial world?

God has immeasurably more for us in the confines of this natural and normal world. God does not want us to walk further into the future alone, but with Him and His presence, with others and His people, and with His power.

HIS PRESENCE

Jesus promises us that, as we journey with Him and go about the life that He has called us to, He "will be with us always, even to the end of the age".[1]

But what does Jesus mean when He tells the disciples that He will be with them? How did the disciples understand God's presence up to this point? The story of Abraham is the story of God's promised presence with a man. Abraham spoke with God and experienced His presence as a man talking with a friend. It didn't matter what was happening around Abraham or whom he was encountering, be it King Melchizedek or the Angel of the Lord at Moriah. The reality of this relationship was that he spoke directly and often in person with God.

In Genesis 18 Abraham has a conversation with God in which he engages Him in "back and forth" banter. This relationship with God was real.

In Exodus 33:11 we are told that Moses also had face-to-face conversations with God. I have this image of Moses sitting chatting to God over a chess game in a close, intimate conversation. I find it amazing that God is willing to struggle with us. Here God is present just as He was with Abraham, yet He changes the experience to suit Moses.

Jacob had a similar experience. Finding himself alone one evening while moving house, he is approached by a strange, unknown presence. This presence is God in human form. This God-man wrestles with Jacob all night and as the sun starts to come up the man touches Jacob's hip and wrenches it in its socket. Jacob demands to know who the unknown man is. The God-man replies, "Why do you ask my name?" Then He calls His anointing down on him there and then. Jacob names the place Peniel ("face of God"), saying, "It is because I saw God face to face, and yet my life was spared".[2]

Abraham spoke with God face to face.

Moses sat face to face with God.

Jacob wrestled face to face with a God-man.

God wants to meet us in the grass roots of life.

Isaiah 41:10 says, "So do not fear, for I am with you; do not be dismayed, for I am your God. I will strengthen you and help you; I will uphold you with my righteous right hand."

The Bible also says, "The eyes of the Lord search the whole earth in order to strengthen those whose hearts are fully committed to him" (2 Chronicles 16:9, NLT). The Lord doesn't miss a thing. He knows your ups and your downs; He knows the pressure you are under and the weight on your shoulders; He knows everything about you. He knows every thought you have.

Despite all the ways God's people have failed Him, despite all the ways *we* have failed Him, God still wants an intimate relationship and longs to be with us.

HIS PEOPLE

I was recently at my son's school sports day and he was due to run the 25 metres. Everyone lined up on the starting line and the gun was fired and they were was off. As the children ran, parents stood around the track shouting encouragement to their children. Some parents were even shouting encouragement to other people's children.

"COME ON, ISAAC, YOU CAN DO IT! KEEP GOING; DON'T LOOK BACK; THE END IS IN SIGHT. PRESS ON, GO ON, YOU'RE DOING SO WELL. KEEP LOOKING AHEAD; GO, GO, GO!"

The buzz around a racetrack, whether it be on the junior-school playing field or at the Olympics, is immense: you can't beat it.

During the Olympics our family were able to go and see the Paralympic swimming relay. Swimming is hard enough without doing it with special needs or a disability. We were all more than impressed. But there was one race that simply blew me away. It was a four-swimmer relay. The race started and we were doing well; I think we were coming in around sixth place with the first two swimmers of the race. But something shifted in the crowd as the third swimmer raced and we realized she had moved the UK up from sixth to third place. The final swimmer jumped in and we were all amazed: she moved us up to second place and climbing. Everyone in the room who was able was up on their feet screaming, really screaming. I found myself shouting, "You go, girl, you beauty!" The sound of the crowd yelling was louder than anything I had ever heard. Our team came in first, and the spectators were ecstatic.

GOLD!

Paul paints a picture of a crowd. Not one shouting only when we're going to win, but a crowd that's always shouting and cheering us on. It's this great crowd that God has given us to cheer us on to go further than we can imagine.

> *Therefore, since we are surrounded by such a huge crowd of witnesses to the life of faith, let us strip off every weight that slows us down, especially the sin that so easily trips us up. And let us run with endurance the race God has set before us.*
> **Hebrews 12:1 (NLT)**

Imagine this for a moment. You actually have a crowd cheering you on all the time. Paul calls it a great cloud of witnesses. He is imagining a Roman arena where the races for the early sports events would have been on display. This crowd of witnesses are celebrating as you wake up for a new day, urging you to use the breath that God has given you to pursue the things that He has set out for you.

Imagine your normal day and this crowd shouting:

> *Come on, [insert your name], wake up! It's a new day, new challenges are ahead. We are excited to see how God is going to use you today. We are overjoyed that you have an impact on the world with your smile and humour; your encouragement to others in the small things is great and is actually building confidence in those around you. We love the fact that you are a great friend because you make time for those around you. We love the fact that people see something different in you. We love that God has a plan and we wait with bated breath to see that unfold today. You might see monotony – we see changed lives.*

How would that make you feel about the monotony of life? How would it make you feel about work, family, marriage, neighbours, the place you hang out or spend most of your time? Would it change the way you see what you do, or the impact you have?

For me, this would change my day, week, month, and year. It would almost send me out each day with excitement and a willingness to make a difference for people. I would most probably rethink what I did with parts of my day: I'd rid my life of some commitments; I would certainly run with perseverance, and most of all it would make me focus on Jesus, seeing where He is leading me and how I might serve Him today.

Knowing they were cheering me on would make me keep going and run harder.

Players on a football pitch often say that a home game brings an advantage. A home-field advantage can mean everything in sport. Teams that play at home often have a far better record than those on the road. When teams have someone cheering them on, they can often exceed their natural ability and surprise even themselves.

So you're also surrounded by "a huge cloud of witnesses to this life of faith". Moses is watching you. Abraham is watching you. Jacob is watching you. Ruth is watching you. Deborah is watching you. Peter is watching you. Paul is watching you. And the noise is deafening.

HIS POWER

It's the Lord's desire that the supernatural territory we occupy, the realms of life where we consistently demonstrate His authority, grow larger and more powerful as we pass it on to the next generation.
Bill Johnson of Bethel Church

God gives us His presence by speaking with us; He gives us the church and the cloud of witnesses, and He also gives us His power to be dynamite. It's not by our strength or by our striving but by the work done by Jesus that we are able even to be in this position. As Paul says, "My grace is sufficient for you, for my power is made perfect in weakness. Therefore I will boast all the more gladly about my weaknesses, so that Christ's power may rest on me." It is His power made perfect in us that gives us what we need.

In Zechariah 4:6 God speaks to Zerubbabel, the governor of the Persian province of Judah, saying, "'Not by might nor by power, but by my Spirit,' says the Lord Almighty." It's all about Him and what He gives by the power of the Spirit. Jesus promises to be with you always, through the Spirit who dwells within you to encourage and to empower you. Sometimes you will find yourself speaking and will realize that what you have just said wasn't your words but His. Sometimes you will need wisdom, and the power of the Spirit will give you all you need and you will realize it's nothing to do with you but with Him. We are to "be strong in the Lord and in his mighty power".[3] Paul is telling us that the unlimited power and strength of Jesus is the source of immeasurably more for those who belong to Him.

BENEDICTION AND FINAL GREETING

Paul knew that the gospel, Jesus' death and His resurrection and now the outpouring of the Holy Spirit weren't for some hyper-spiritual life. It wasn't something just for holy days but something for each and every moment. The Hebrews were people who needed to know this more than anyone else. The Hebrews were people with short memories; that's why God constantly reminds them to "remember" what He has done for them. The most frequently recurring word in the first third of the Bible is "remember".

Remember, remember, remember.

God knew they wouldn't, and so the writer of the letter to the Hebrews leaves them with a benediction, or blessing if you prefer. In it he reminds them of the good news of salvation, God's promise of peace, and His promise to equip His people for all that is set before them.

The author writes:

> Now may the God of peace, who through
> the blood of the eternal covenant brought
> back from the dead our Lord Jesus, that
> great Shepherd of the sheep, equip you
> with everything good for doing his will, and
> may he work in us what is pleasing to him,
> through Jesus Christ, to whom be glory for
> ever and ever. Amen.
> Hebrews 13:20–21

PRAYER

*May the God of presence, community, and
power, who has risen from the dead, that
great Shepherd and sustainer of His people,
nurture us and lead us by His own mighty
power, that we may from now and forever
belong to Him, forever be transformed by
His Spirit, forever serve Him, and forever
go His way. May the Lord be gracious to us,
now and for ever.*

AMEN.

Immeasurably More: Small-Group Study

QUESTION: Have you ever been involved with sport? What things have made you disheartened and want to stop?

QUESTION: Are you usually someone who completes a task or someone who is likely to give up if the job gets too hard?

QUESTION: Does knowing that you have others cheering you on in a hard task make it easier for you, or impose a greater pressure to finish?

QUESTION: Do you ever think about what you are going to need to do to make sure you're still a follower of Jesus at the end of your life? What investments might you need to make?

At this point, pray that as we read the passage the Holy Spirit would reveal to us what He is wanting to say through it.

READ: Hebrews 12:1–3

What jumps out from this passage?

Do you notice something you haven't seen before or don't understand?

What is God saying to you in this reading?

QUESTION: The writer to the Hebrews (very possibly Paul) says that they should throw off everything that hinders them. What do you think hinders *you* from running the race of faith?

QUESTION: What are the links for you between running a race and being a Christian for the long term?

QUESTION: The author makes the link between Jesus enduring the cross, His death, and His resurrection as an inspiration to us in running our race. What is it about Jesus that inspires you?

READ: 2 Chronicles 16:9

"For the eyes of the Lord range throughout the earth to strengthen those whose hearts are fully committed to him."

QUESTION: God is searching for people He can strengthen. All He asks is that our hearts are committed to Him. Does it bring you comfort, knowing that if you really want to commit yourself to Him and His race He will be searching for you in order to strengthen you? This is something He is doing without our knowledge.

QUESTION: In what areas do you want God to strengthen you by His Spirit for what lies ahead?

PRAY

Get the group to hold their shoes in their hands as a symbol of the race set before them.

Lord, by Your Spirit we ask You to anoint these feet for the race ahead. May they remain steadfast in the path that You have called them to walk. May they know Your presence when walking into unknown places and Your peace when going into the lives of people who don't know You. May these feet be anointed as holy feet that bring life to the dead pavements all around them. Anoint these feet to take the message of good news to those in need, those who are oppressed, and those needing a miracle. Amen.

EPILOGUE:
THE ENDING

So we come to the end of what is only a foretaste of all that is possible through God's glory and greatness. Life is an adventure, and so is our relationship with Him who gave it to us. Whenever we think we have completed our training in the work of the kingdom, we are reminded with each breath that God has much more in store for us.

It would be like our trying to dress ourselves in Barbie or Action Man clothing. The clothes just don't fit; it would be ridiculous to try. But that's what we try to do with God. We try to limit Him to immeasurably less glory and power than He deserves. As we expand our knowledge of and love for Him, we realize the old ways of describing, seeing, and engaging with the God of immeasurably more are nothing but silly little ideas.

I want to end with a dare. I'm convinced that we don't lose people from the church because we haven't entertained them; we lose them because we haven't challenged them enough. I dare you to actively pursue doing and practising the things that Jesus taught His disciples. If we were seeing miracles every week, then we would see people flocking to the church. I dare you to have enough foolishness to believe that the things Jesus showed His disciples are still what He wants His church to do. Pray for the sick, wait on His Spirit daily, ask Him to fill you so that you might be empowered to have a wider imagination for the world around you. Focus on what the Lord has done and not on what He hasn't done yet, and allow your concept of God to expand, grow, and become a wide-angle panoramic view of His kingdom. Be daring enough to sit with others in the unknowing of Holy Saturday while holding on to the hope of the resurrection that will come.

I dare you to worship a much **HIGHER**, bigger, and more expansive God who is **CLOSER** than you could ever imagine. I dare you to spend as much time as possible waiting on Him to take you **DEEPER** into His living water. I dare you to pursue a **WIDER** and more extensive work of the Spirit as you seek justice, pray for the sick, and set the captives free. And I dare you to be led **FURTHER** into what God has for you and His beautiful church.

Our Father in heaven, may Your kingdom come on earth as it is in heaven.
Amen.

NOTES

Foreword
1. This story is adapted from Simon Ponsonby, *More: How to have more of the Spirit when we have everything in Christ*, David C Cook, 2009.

Epigraph
A. W. Tozer, *The Pursuit of God.*

Movement One, Higher
Chapter 1: A Miniature God
1. J. I. Packer, *Knowing God*, London: Hodder & Stoughton, 1977.
2. Romans 11:33–34, NASB.
3. A. W. Tozer, *The Knowledge of the Holy*, Cambridge: Lutterworth Press, 1965. Used with permission.
4. Tozer, *The Knowledge of the Holy*. Used with permission.
5. Jude 24–25.
6. 1 Timothy 1:17.

Chapter 2: Regaining Wonder
1. N. T. Wright, "The Bible and Christian Imagination", lecture at Seattle Pacific University, 18 May 2005. Used with permission. Transcript at http://www.spu.edu/depts/uc/response/summer2k5/features/imagination.asp
2. Tozer, *The Knowledge of the Holy*. Used with permission.
3. James Christian, *Philosophy: An Introduction to the Art of Wondering*, New York: Holt McDougal, 1973, page 380.
4. Isaiah 40:26.
5. Hermann Hagedorn, "Starry Night", from *Combat at Midnight: A Book of Poems*, New York: The John Day Company, 1940.
6. Voltaire (François-Marie Arouet, 1694–1778).
7. John Piper, *Think*, Wheaton, IL: Crossway Books, 2010, page 194.

Chapter 3: Too Familiar
1. A. W. Tozer, *Worship: The Missing Jewel*, Harrisburg, PA: Christian Publications, 1992, page 21.
2. Rob Bell, *Rediscovering Wonder* short film, http://www.youtube.com/watch?v=dF-V_t_NSHw
3. Prayer by Matt Long of the Bless Network, a Christian mission agency working in mainland Europe through gap-year discipleship schemes, short-term mission teams, prayer weekends, and a web-based prayer network. Bless operates through its links with local churches in France, Croatia, Spain, and the Netherlands. Prayer used with permission from the author.

Movement Two, Closer
Chapter 1: Does My Religion Look Big In This?
1. C. S. Lewis, *Mere Christianity*, London: Fontana, 1955 (first published 1952).
2. John Ortberg, *God Is Closer Than You Think*, Grand Rapids, MI: Zondervan, 2005, page 15.
3. Mark Driscoll, *Religion Saves*, http://www.youtube.com/watch?v=LEpU_gAuTQc.
4. Mark Driscoll, from "We don't need Religion; we need Jesus", https://marshill.

com/media/luke/jesus-and-religion/ajax_transcript?lang=en, used with permission.
5. http://www.huffingtonpost.com/steve-mcswain/how-to-know-god_b_875204.html

Chapter 2: Beyond Religion

1. Max Lucado, *Grace*, Nashville, TN: Thomas Nelson, 2014, page 4.
2. Brennan Manning, *The Ragamuffin Gospel: Good News for the Bedraggled, Beat-Up, and Burnt Out*, Portland, OR: Multnomah Press, 2005, page 17.
3. Manning, *The Ragamuffin Gospel*.
4. Manning, *The Ragamuffin Gospel*, page 13.

Chapter 3: God is Closer Than You Think

1. Rob Bell, *Rediscovering Wonder*.
2. George MacLeod, *Daily Readings with George MacLeod*, Glasgow: Wild Goose Publications, 2004, page 106. Copyright © George MacLeod. Used with permission.
3. Isaiah 30:21.
4. James 4:8, ESV.
5. Ortberg, *God Is Closer Than You Think*, page 13.
6. Prayer by Matt Long of Bless Network. Used with permission.

Movement Three, Deeper
Chapter 1: Roots

1. Lewis, *Mere Christianity*.
2. Ephesians 3:17.
3. Prayer by Matt Long of Bless Network. Used with permission.
4. Rick Warren, *The Purpose Driven Life*, Grand Rapids, MI: Zondervan, 2003.

Chapter 2: Sitting – Waiting

1. Luke 5:4 (MSG).

Chapter 3: Filled, Not Shrivelling

1. http://www.kingschurchbeverley.org/johnarnott.html
2. Judges 14:6.
3. 2 Chronicles 24:20.
4. Judges 3:10.
5. Judges 6:34.
6. Matthew 1:18.
7. Luke 3:22.
8. Philippians 3:8.
9. Acts 2:38.
10. Extract taken from "Oceans (Where Feet May Fail)". Words and Music by Matt Crocker, Joel Houston & Salomon Ligthelm © 2012 Hillsong Music Publishing (APRA) CCLI: 6428767. Used by permission.
11. C. S. Lewis, *The Weight of Glory*, New York: HarperOne, 2001, page 187.

Movement Four, Wider
Chapter 1: Wider In Us

1. Psalm 77:7.
2. Psalm 77:13–14.
3. ESV.
4. NIV.
5. Extract taken from an interview with Walter Brueggemann by Krista Tippett, copyright © 2013 On Being http://onbeing.org. Used with permission.

6. Walter Brueggemann, *Prophetic Imagination*, Minneapolis, MN: Fortress Press, 2001.

7. Extract taken from the song "Consuming Fire" by Tim Hughes, copyright © 2002 Thankyou Music/Adm. By Capitol CMG Publishing excl. UK & Europe, adm. by Integritymusic.com, a division of David C Cook songs@integritymusic.com. Used by permission.

8. Based on Ephesians 3:20–21, MSG.

Chapter 2: Naturally Supernatural

1. Gary Best Page, *Naturally Supernatural: God May Be Closer Than You Think*, Cape Town, SA: Vineyard International Publishing, 2007, page 15.

2. Matthew 7:7, NLT.

3. R. T. Kendall, *The Anointing*, London: Hodder & Stoughton, 1998, page 9.

4. Kendall, *The Anointing*, page 9.

5. Martyn Lloyd-Jones, *The Sovereign Spirit*, Carol Stream, IL: Harold Shaw, 1986, pages 31–32.

Chapter 3: Wider For The World

1. Romans 8:11.

2. Philippians 2:6–8.

3. 1 Corinthians 12:4–6.

4. 1 Corinthians 12:7–11.

5. Lewis, *The Weight of Glory*, page 187.

6. 1 Corinthians 12:31.

7. 1 Corinthians 14:1, NLT.

Movement Five, Further

Chapter 1: Forward Through Disbelief

1. Pete Greig, *God on Mute: Engaging the Silence of Unanswered Prayer*, Eastbourne: Kingsway, 2007, page 237.

2. An extract from an ancient homily for Holy Saturday, used by some churches in their Holy Saturday liturgy.

3. Oscar Cullmann, *Christ and Time: The Primitive Christian Conception of Time and History*, Philadelphia, PA: Westminster Press, 1964.

4. 2 Corinthians 7:6.

5. Isaiah 43:2.

6. Psalm 91:1–2, ESV.

Chapter 2: Further Into The World

1. Acts 1:8.

2. N. T. Wright, *Paul for Tomorrow's World*, sermon at St Andrews Presbyterian Church, Newport Beach, CA. Used with permission. http://www.sapres.org/sermons/index.html

3. Gordon Fee, *God's Empowering Presence: The Holy Spirit in the Letters of Paul*, Grand Rapids, MI: Baker Academic, 2009.

4. 1 Corinthians 2:4–5.

Chapter 3: More In The Normal And The Mundane

1. Matthew 28:20.

2. Genesis 32:30.

3. Ephesians 6:10.

ACKNOWLEDGMENTS

Image credits

p. 4   Jag_cz, Shutterstock.com
p. 10   Galyna Andrushko, Shutterstock.com
p. 30   Cris Rogers
p. 39   art_frei, Shutterstock.com
p. 43   Sylvie Corriveau, Shutterstock.com
p. 51   McCarthy's PhotoWorks, Shutterstock.com
p. 104 Cosmin-Constantin Sava, 123RF.com
p. 108 Tanvi Malik, edited by Mark Steel
p. 116 Eric Isselee, Shutterstock.com
p. 120 Ozerov Alexander, Shutterstock.com
p. 125 Cris Rogers
p. 141 antart, Shutterstock.com
p. 144 Yuriy Khimanin
p. 157 Griffin Keller
p. 162 phloen, Shutterstock.com
p. 187 Cris Rogers
p. 196 Casey Fyfe
p. 198 Mark Steel
p. 234 Taylor Leopold
p. 248 Lukasz Szmigiel

Additional text credits

Extracts pages 73, 78, and 134 taken from Mere Christianity by C.S. Lewis, copyright © C.S. Lewis Pte. Ltd. 1942, 1943, 1952. Extracts reprinted with permission.

Extracts pages 169 and 220 taken from The Weight of Glory by C.S. Lewis, copyright © C.S. Lewis Pte. Ltd. 1949. Extracts reprinted by permission.

Extracts pages 93, 96, and 97 taken from *The Ragamuffin Gospel: Good News for the Bedraggled, Beat-Up, and Burnt Out* by Brenna Manning, copyright © 1990 by Brennan Manning. Used by permission of WaterBrook Multnomah, an imprint of the Crown Publishing Group, a division of Random House LLC. All rights reserved.

Previous books by this author:

Naked Christianity: Helping Young People Grasp Issues of Faith (Kevin Mayhew, 2004, out of print)

Am I a Freak? (Kevin Mayhew, 2005)

A Monkey's Orientation: A Book About Holiness (Authentic, 2008)

Practising Resurrection: The Church Being Jesus' Hands, Feet and Heart (Authentic, 2010)

The Bible Book by Book (Monarch, 2012)